Pac-Man Life

Tony Moreno

Publisher contact information:
Book Writer Corner
433 Walnut Ct Pittsburgh PA 15237, USA
e-mail: info@bookwritercorner.com
https://bookwritercorner.com/
412-274-7334
Paperback ISBN: 978-1-960815-57-6
Hardcover ISBN: 978-1-960815-58-3

Notice to the Reader: Concepts, principles, techniques, and opinions presented in this manual are provided as possible considerations. The application, use, or adoption of any concepts, principles, techniques, or opinions contained in this manual are the risk of the individual or organization who makes that decision. The authors or their heirs or beneficiaries shall not be held liable or responsible for any application, use, or adoption of any part of this manual.

Dedication

This book is dedicated to all the people who have made it possible for me to last for over 40 years, learning, teaching, and sharing information with others.

Thank you to my mom and dad, Aurora and Tony Moreno, my sister Gloria and my four kids, Ryan, Kim, Desiree, and Marcus, for always being there for me.

My 12 grandkids, who gave me the enjoyment of watching them grow up and who I expect will continue doing well in life.
To my friends, family, and professional colleagues, thank you all. There aren't enough words to express my gratitude to all of you.

This book is also dedicated to the kids and young adults who aren't as fortunate as I was and who must take on the world with or without loving parents ...

God bless all of you.

CONTENTS

Introduction

I've been on the frontline of law enforcement for over 45 years, entering the police academy in 1975. Although I retired 15 years ago, I have stayed close to law enforcement and, to this day, continue to write and train frontline law enforcement professionals throughout the world.

My claim to fame was working for gangs in south/central Los Angeles and doing it while driving a yellow, 4-door Plymouth Fury police car.

I was assigned to the LAPD citywide gang detail and drove that car for 5 years, having about four different partners during that time. One night, the screenwriter for a controversial movie about gangs rode along with my partner and me to see how LAPD gang cops worked. When we were done, he did learn a couple of things, but I think the thing that really impressed him was how we got along with the gang members.

I think he believed that because of the contentious nature of our relationship, cops and gang members did not get along. Most of the time that is true, but it's not all of the time, and due to the nature of the beast, there are times when you actually trust and rely on each other. There are times when you actually see the desperation, the betrayal, and the evil in people. Unless you've been in that situation, you won't know what that really feels like.

Some of you know the feeling and take it as part of the job. There's more to it than simply good versus evil.

In 1987, the movie "Colors" came out, and I've been the famous "Pac-Man" ever since.

This book is a compilation of lessons I have learned, quotes, and principles I have used over the years in my work, my training, and the books I've written. For the most part, the principles and philosophies have not changed, and I don't expect they will. Some may sound somewhat familiar, but they are "original" to what I preach and do come from my teachings. These are things that I actually believe in and use in my training and books.

If there is one thing I have noticed in law enforcement training trends over the past 45 years that I've been conducting training, it is that there is more of an emphasis on "mental wellness." I know I have incorporated "mental wellness" into most of my classes, and it is totally appropriate … and needed.

I think some law enforcement people resent being told how to maintain "mental wellness" by a doctor or someone else who has never been in their situations or done the job themselves.

I have received very good feedback from my training because I have been right there in the trenches with everyone else, and I discuss what has worked for me … and what hasn't. Many of them are in Chapter 6 of this book, "Your Personal Battle."

I hope you enjoy the book and you pass on the knowledge, ideas, and insights you may get from reading it.

Do well and enjoy your career … enjoy your life.

Like my business card says, "Making people safer and more effective." I forgot to add "and happier, too."

"My Ten Principles of Crime Fighting"

1. Evil People Do Exist.
For various reasons, some people are just mean, evil, and/or heartless when it comes to the treatment of their fellow man. Law enforcement's job is to keep law-abiding people "safe" from those who intend to victimize and prey on others.

"The heaviest crime is heartlessness."- Confucius.

2. Fighting Evil Is an Ugly Job.
Stepping in to stop a crime or an act of evil is not a pleasant sight because it is not a pleasant business. Many times, those committing evil acts are not going to comply or submit to law enforcement, and when that happens, you have chaos. Law enforcement must deal with that chaos because that is their job ... and who else will?

"We expect them (the police) to keep the bad guys out of our businesses, cars, and houses ... out of our face. We want them to take care of the problem. We just don't want to see how it's done."– Charles H. Webb, PhD

3. Law Enforcement Stands Between Good And Evil.
The reason that evil doesn't completely overrun society is that there are those who take a stand and won't allow it. The best people are sworn to it, those people being law enforcement. If you soften, lessen, or take the law enforcement to influence away, the criminal wins and society loses.

"People sleep peaceably at night only because rough men stand ready to do violence on their behalf." – George Orwell.

4. Law Enforcement Must Be A Deterrent To Crime.
To a criminal, law enforcement must be a legitimate deterrent that discourages criminal acts. If your job is to seek out and deter crime, that is what you are going to do. That is law enforcement's most important role in order to keep people safe.

"Intimidation doesn't really exist if you're in the right frame of mind"– Kobe Bryant.

5. Criminals Understand And Use Violence.

Violence and the threat of violence give the criminal power. It gives them power because the average person doesn't live with the threat of violence in their life. The average person has been taught not to use violence as currency. They have been taught to be better than that.

"Education is the vaccine for violence."– Edward James Olmos.

6. Criminals Prey On Weakness.

Intimidation can expose a weakness. Criminals and gang members know that. That is why a gang member's behavior is symbolically bold, loud, and brazen. They operate on the assumption that disinterest and apathy are rampant in the community because people want to mind their own business.

"The first thing a pirate does when he walks into a room is notice the other pirates."– Unknown Pirate.

7. Perception Is Reality.

Criminals act on what they perceive. If you seem weak or vulnerable, you are. If you are unaware of your surroundings, you are. If you seem strong and confident, you are. Criminals act based on their perceptions … right time … wrong time … right person … wrong person. It's what they are thinking at the time that matters.

"We don't see things as they are. We see things as we are." – Anais Nin.

8. A Predator Only Fears Another Predator.

In the gang and criminal world, very few people stand up to criminal acts unless they are the ones being victimized. Law enforcement is an exception to that rule because one of law enforcement's roles is to seek out the "evil-doers." They prey on predators.

"To protect the sheep, you have to catch the wolf, and it takes a wolf to catch a wolf." – Detective Alonzo Harris, Training Day.

9. The Stronger The Law Enforcement Leadership, The Safer The Community.

When law enforcement has the safety of the community as its top priority, the community is safer. Law enforcement must not lose sight of its goal of public safety and must not be distracted by certain incidents or situations, relying on its first responsibility ... public safety.

"People don't care how much you know until they know how much you care."– Steve Gutzler.

10. The Safer the Officers, The Safer the Community.

As the community works with, supports, and ensures the safety of its law enforcement officers, it ensures its own safety. It only makes sense that the safer its officers, the safer the people and the community are as they work together towards that goal.

"If people didn't want the police, they wouldn't call ... and they keep on calling and calling."- Tony "Pac-Man" Moreno.

Chapter 1 – The Job

"Blessed Are the Peacemakers, For They Shall Be Called the Children of God" – Mathew 5:9

"It's not how much you do; it's what you do."

I learned as a young police officer not to "spin my wheels." In other words, you can look as busy as hell, but is anything important being accomplished? Do you do memorable things? Do you do things that last in your mind and in the mind of others? Do you make a difference to somebody?

Here's an example.

I used to interview gang members that were in custody in the LA County Jail to identify them and talk to them about what was going on in the gang world. I was working alongside the LA County Sheriff's Operation Safe Streets deputies, who at the time had an office in the jail. They were kind enough to give me a desk and allow me to work with them. I was focusing on gang members from the city of Los Angeles.

This operation worked so well that I expanded it to Sybil Brand Institute, which was the women's jail also controlled by LA County Sheriffs. I would go there one day a week and interview female gang members and other inmates.

One day a deputy told me an inmate wanted to speak to me. The deputy brought her into the interview room. The inmate had been arrested for prostitution and would be released in two days. She said she could solve a murder if I agreed to help her out.

This inmate was only 20 years old and seemed pretty frightened. She was from Northern California, far away from Los Angeles. She left home and came to Los Angeles looking for a job and maybe hoping to catch a dream as a movie star while she was still young and good-looking.

She ran into a pimp and was no match for his game and salesmanship, and in no time, she was turning tricks for him and totally under his control. She was threatened and abused and couldn't leave out of fear. Then she got arrested.

She was serving a short jail term, and when released, the pimp would be waiting outside the jail to scoop her up and put her back to working on the street. Meanwhile, her mother made arrangements to drive her back home, but she didn't think the pimp was going to let that happen. She needed help.

She gave me information on the murder, and that turned out to be solid, solving a "whodunit" type of homicide. Two days later, when she was to be released, my partner and I showed up along with the pimp. As she was being released, we detained him "conducting a prostitution investigation," making sure that he couldn't follow or catch up to her and her mom. She was free.

I don't know what happened to her, but I do remember that it was one of those moments that made me feel I had done something worthwhile. It didn't show up in the newspapers, nor did it count as a felony arrest on our recap or even result in a citizen's letter of commendation, but in my heart, I knew we had done something very important.

That, to me, was worth more than a bunch of mediocre arrests some officers seem to thrive on. I will always remember that day, and hopefully, in your career, you'll have enough of them to keep you going just like it did for me.

I felt very important on that day.

"The strongest asset you have working gangs is your attitude."

One of the most important weapons that we have in our "arsenal" for life is our attitude. Our attitude can determine whether we succeed or fail, win or lose, progress or digress.

Our attitude is a product of our experiences, perceptions, biases, and mental dexterity. We ultimately decide how we travel our own road, and our attitude is our traveling music.

Our attitude can also burden us with negativity, complacency, and arrogance. In many walks of life, that's a mixture made for trouble, even death.

I was reading a book that had its main topics dealing with the term's *paradigm* and *paradigm* shift.

A "paradigm" is basically a model, example, mold, or pattern, a stereotypical example. A "*paradigm* shift" is a drastic change in that mold or pattern. The book examines the theory of *paradigm* shifts within us as individuals.

In other words, for me would mean looking and living outside the "Tony Moreno paradigm" I have created for myself. To myself and a few people close to me, I am predictable in that I think, feel, act and live a certain way. I am the Tony Moreno paradigm, and I will be that way today, tomorrow, and the day after that.

Now in a lot of ways, that's not a bad thing because I happen to think that Tony Moreno is a decent guy most of the time. But maybe I can improve or at least experiment in a couple of areas of my life. You know, try living outside the Tony Moreno box.

Here's a good example of what it means. I love music. I also like to dance but don't have total confidence in it for a couple of reasons. First off, my body isn't made for dancing, and secondly, a good male dancer outshines everyone on the floor because the women swoon over him, the bastard. I'm good at a few things, and to me dancing isn't one of them. That's why if I am somewhere and I know I'm going to be dancing, my foreplay sounds like, "Another beer, please."

If I sign up for a ballroom dance class, I am experiencing a "*paradigm shift*" to the max. I am changing and adjusting the "Tony Moreno paradigm." I am also changing my attitude toward dancing and towards myself.

We all have our experiences, prejudices, perceptions, fears, biases, feelings, and impressions. We all have our attitudes. Sometimes it's good for us to "overhaul" or "check" ourselves. That's how we learn and evolve. That's how we can best experience life itself. You will be the last person to know if you have gone stale. Don't let it happen.

Sometimes you just have to step outside your comfort zone. See what's there and learn more about yourself. Feeling crappy about lost love? Step outside your *paradigm* and gain some strength you didn't know was there.

The weight of the world is on your shoulders? A minor change in your attitude or a *paradigm* shift can do wonders. You have to get yourself out of your funk you do.

So, when you are around some friends or loved ones, sit back, smile, look up at the sky, and let out a real loud howl, "Ah-ooh!"

And when someone looks over at you, notices that shit-eating grin on your face and the fire in your eyes, and says to you, "Are you OK?"

You can say, "I'm fine; just checking my attitude."

"You Can Be Right at The Wrong Time. Understand the Game ...."

In Northeast Division, there was a very notable shooting of a young child that got the people and the news media pretty excited, and rightfully so. It wasn't our case, so we watched it from a distance because working the gangs in the area. We were floating in and out of the division, working our own caseload and busy looking for some wanted suspects.

Without getting into the specifics of the case, these gang members in a dead-end street fired on a vehicle that tried to leave the street, killing a young passenger in the vehicle. There was a lot of speculation as to the circumstances of the shooting itself, and eventually, a suspect was identified and arrested. They even held a press conference.

An informant contacted us and told us the wrong suspect had been arrested in the shooting. This informant, who was really good, insisted we had the wrong guy. My partner and I talked it over and spoke with the homicide team who had the case and with our supervisor to let him know what was up.

When we told them of our informant and his information, they kind of blew us off. We even ran our information by the deputy district attorney on the case, and like them, he seemed resentful of us for sticking our noses into their case. It didn't matter to me as long as the "right" suspect was arrested and the case was solved. I didn't have "a dog in the fight," as the saying goes. I just thought that it was interesting that we had bruised a few egos by bringing up our information and sharing it. No one was trying to sabotage anyone's case.

A weird thing happened a few days later. The attorney of the suspect they had arrested in the case produced a video from a gas station in Northern California, a few hundred miles away, that showed the suspect buying gasoline right about the same time that the shooting had occurred in Loa Angeles. It was the perfect alibi … and on video.

They released the suspect because he was the wrong suspect, and all eyes turned toward us. It was as if we were some jealous assholes who jinxed their case just to make them look bad. Nothing could be further from the truth, but that's not how everyone who was working on that case saw it.

What surprised me about that whole scenario was how fragile some egos are and how hard it is for some people to admit they were wrong.

It was so hard to admit they were wrong that they had to blame us for it. There was nothing wrong with how they had worked their case; they just had the wrong suspect. That happens, and that wasn't our fault.

The detectives eventually solved the case and arrested the right suspect … the same suspect our informant said it was. So that didn't help our relationship with those detectives very much, but at a certain point, you have to put egos and bruises aside and move on because we all still have a job to do.

I don't know what would have happened with the case if that video didn't show up, but it did, and the right suspect was found guilty in connection with the shooting.

It just goes to show that you can be right at the wrong time, so be strong and stand up for yourself, your position, and your information. Sometimes it all comes down to if someone wants to believe you or not. All you can do is the right thing … that's your job and your responsibility.

"If you're going 20 mph and everyone around you is going 10 mph, you're not going to be a very popular person. Always remember that …."

In a highly competitive profession like law enforcement, you are normally expected to do "your share" of the work, and usually, most people do. However, sometimes there are situations where doing more than your share is not appreciated.

I've experienced this a few times in my career, and at first, it was hard for me to understand and accept.

Usually, this happens when a person walks into a situation where the work quality or level is not optimal. In a couple of situations, I encountered, the workload and quality were mediocre at best. In my opinion, it was a mediocre culture encouraged by mediocre people doing mediocre work. Everybody in that situation was satisfied with it, so it wasn't going to change or get any better.

When it first happened to me, I couldn't understand why I was making enemies when all I was trying to do was learn, work hard, and get better at what I was doing. Not everyone had the same goals.

Luckily for me, I had a solid supervisor who knew there was a problem and thought that I might be able to effect a change in the unit.

We were one of four squads in a division that had about 40 detectives and officers. Our squad also had a couple of "workers" already doing good stuff.

I was adding to that team and their cause. My supervisor knew that he just had to give me a partner that would go along with what I was doing, and we'd be successful.

Once I found a suitable partner, we were off and rolling, and the other guys in our squad were also handling their business. Our squad was actually putting the other squads to shame, but that wasn't our intention.

We were making arrests, helping the divisional detectives around the city, and helping each other out.

Everything was fine until we had a squad meeting where everyone met face-to-face to discuss crimes, wanted suspects, and other businesses in the gang world. I really didn't know there was a problem until one of the older detectives in the division made a comment. He said, "I don't know what's wrong with some of the people in this unit, running around like they are CRASH units." CRASH units were the divisional and bureau gang units at the time.

Up until this time, I would get an occasional comment from someone in the other squads. I just didn't pay attention because I stayed busy. Since that arrow was obviously fired at me, I couldn't help but respond, "What's wrong with that? Maybe more of us should run around like that."

The room went quiet. There was no legitimate response to my comment. To be honest, I actually blurted that out because I was caught off guard, but it pissed me off. I had been married for a few years at that time, so I knew, "Don't criticize me unless I do something wrong." I never heard anything more about this.

There were a couple of reasons why I survived this squad meeting and continued to work and be happy. First off, my supervisor was supportive of our work. He was married, so he also knew the philosophy, "Let me know when I do something wrong." He did what a good supervisor is supposed to do. Because our hearts and efforts were in the right place, he protected us. It sounds simple, but it's not and is important.

My partners and the other members of our squad were also protected by our supervisor. We were safe, and we were very successful. That is essential in transforming or improving a culture.

If you are ever in a situation like this, hopefully, you have a "strong" supervisor who backs your good work all the way.

Until then, let me know when I do something wrong.

"Being a cop is like coaching. Everybody can do a better job, but no one ever does."

I've been around sports my entire life, and as I have gotten older, I notice that a lot of fans like to criticize the players and coaches.

It's like that in most sports, and it seems the fans get more spoiled and more critical, taking for granted the skill, effort, talent, and intelligence it takes to be successful at high levels of competition.

I was at a hockey game and had to suffer listening to a big-mouth, jersey-wearing fan-boy loudly proclaiming this player should skate faster, and that player should hit harder. Yet the big mouth probably can't even stand up on skates, much less skate and perform close to the level of the people he is so loudly criticizing.

Police work draws much of the same type of criticism. Critics usually appear when something goes wrong, or controversy arises. They are usually people who can't do the job themselves, and if they could, it wouldn't be near the high level of the professionals who do it successfully on a regular basis. They can also be people who will elevate their reputation or prestige at someone else's expense.

As police critics go, it seems like I would stop and throw rocks at every barking dog. As I matured and developed some wisdom ...

and patience, I learned to try and consider the source and remind myself that most police critics probably have an agenda and couldn't do my job as well as I did it.

One night working patrol, my partner, who was a young probationary officer, and I decided to have our code-7 (lunch) at a Chinese restaurant that was located in a sketchy area downtown. It was great food, but if you went there after dark, you were living dangerously.

We parked our black and white police vehicle in front of the location in a red-zone parking curb right in front of the window we were seated at so we could see it and get to it fast if we needed to. Although a great restaurant, it had a very small parking lot for its patrons.

As my trainee and I was eating, a guy I would describe as a successful, upper-crust, arrogant yuppie-type approached us with a beautiful woman at his side. He says, "Excuse me, officers, but what gives you the right to park in a red zone when a tax-paying citizen like myself has to park only where it is legal?"

I turned to him and said, 'Well, as you can see, it's dark outside. If we took up one of the legal parking spots in the lot and you had nowhere to park, you would have to park around the corner down the dark street. In this neighborhood and at this late hour, there's a good chance that someone would have approached you, slapped you around, and who knows what he would have done with the beautiful woman you are with.

Hopefully, he would only take her purse and belongings. So, to save you that embarrassment and inconvenience, I decided to park in the red."

He and his lady friend left speechless. My rookie probationer looked at me and could only say, "Wow."

Unfortunately, most of your critics won't be handled as "easily," and though you may hear the criticisms, have some consolation that the critic couldn't do your job. Being critical makes people feel good about themselves, and that's about it.

"If you're good at what you do, you're going to make enemies. To make them go away, keep being good at what you do."

In law enforcement, if you are good at what you do, you are going to make enemies. I'm not talking about the criminals or people on the other side of the law. I'm talking about people on "your side of the fence." They can be co-workers, colleagues, and members of a peer group and not necessarily someone in a superior or subordinate relationship. It is usually someone that makes you ask yourself, 'What's his or her problem? I have no issue with them.'

This is a competitive field, and whatever success you may have is overshadowing someone else's performance, or that's the perception they have. I had a situation where I wasn't trying to show anybody up or make anyone look bad; I was just doing my job as I normally did. In this particular scenario, other members of this unit were cruising along at 20 miles per hour, and I was going more like 30 mph. They didn't see it as my success, making the entire unit look good. They felt I was making them look bad, which was not my intention. Luckily in this situation, I had a good supervisor who was very supportive, and that really helped me. He knew I loved my job and was doing good work, and as my boss, he had no complaints.

Analyzing that situation, the guys didn't like me because I didn't "fit in" and wouldn't do my work at "their" speed. What it really boiled down to, I had a higher commitment level than they did, and it made them look bad. It was not my intention, but it was now my problem. I had a decision to make. Do I slow my roll, try to fit in, and go 20 miles per hour? Or do I continue my work and let them deal with their own insecurities and mediocre work ethic?

I decided to be true to who I was and continued to work hard at being a good gang cop. I was actually motivated by my critics, and that's what they were on a regular basis, my critics. In the middle of this private war with other members of this unit, a strange thing happened. I kept working to get better and made good arrests, even helping other people with their cases.

Then it happened; the backbiting and criticism stopped. To continue the criticism would shine the light on the pettiness and negative energy that was being thrown my way. I shut them down by doing the very same work that got them started on me to begin with. I didn't set out to do that and didn't really know how to do that, but it happened.

I learned a valuable lesson. Some people won't like you for whatever reason they may have. If it comes down to making someone "look bad" and your intentions are honorable, you just want to be good at what you do. Keep doing what you do and at the level you are doing it, and make yourself better. You only need a few key supporters in life, not everyone.

As I look back on my career and my life, it's amazing the number of detractors that gave me the motivation to become good at what I was doing. A big "thank you" to all the haters out there.

As soccer star Cristiano Ronaldo says, "Sometimes you need the enemy ..."

"A good hitter focuses on the pitch, not the crowd. A good cop does the same thing."

With all of the negative energy swirling around law enforcement nowadays, it's easy to get down and lose the hunger we all had when we were young puppies starting out in the battle between good and evil.

In Southern California, it seemed as though there was always some type of controversy or issue going on with law enforcement. So in a way, it became a part of the life of a police officer.

It forced me to learn how to block out the distractions and issues that might affect some law enforcement officers but didn't directly affect me.

I understood I could be one citizen contact, one tactical situation, or one bad decision (in the media's eyes) from appearing on the front page of the Los Angeles Times or on the evening news. I was aware of that fact, but determined to keep that in the back of my mind and do my duty without that fear making me uneasy or creating any self-doubt.

If you have ever played baseball or softball, you know that when you are batting, you are so focused on the pitcher and the pitch coming at you that you block out all other distractions like the sound of the crowd, the gravity of the situation, or the runners on the move. Any of those things can distract you from the objective of hitting the ball.

When working in law enforcement, if you allow it, there are many things that can interfere with your focus on the job. You may have a sick child at home, a difficult case coming up in court, or are in the process of losing a relationship, but there are times when all that must be put aside.

When pulling a traffic violator over to issue a citation, approaching the front door on a radio call, or walking down the tier in a correctional facility that houses violent gang members, the focus must be on what you are doing. All of your senses must be in tune with the goal you are trying to accomplish. I believe you can practice and sharpen that skill of focusing on the task at hand.

In fact, there were times when I enjoyed being at work because it allowed me an escape from things bothering me in my personal life.

I could always trust my mind to block out distractions and focus on work.

At the present time, many current and former law enforcement officers believe things are so bad that no one can do any work. Yet, great arrests are still being made, great cases are being prosecuted, and many citizens have good experiences with law enforcement.

The suicide rate among cops was high 25 years ago, and it still is now. Divorce rates are traditionally high with law enforcement officers, along with PTSD, medical issues, and mental stressors. It boils down to the power of your mind and the control of perception, and of course, training your mind how to focus.

Train your mind to focus. It is to your benefit in the long run.

"Your expertise isn't determined by what you know. It's determined by who you help make better."

Most young officers want to become knowledgeable and effective. When it comes to knowing your gang, you'd like to be the person that people come to when it comes to knowing "who is who in the zoo," so to speak.

Back in the late '70s and early 80's, there was a lot of competition among law enforcement officers "to know the gang." There's great benefit in knowing a gang, especially if they are very active in the crimes they are committing and if they are committing them in other places.

In the early '80s, cocaine was coming into South Los Angeles, being "rocked up" by gangsters and distributed all over the United States. This meant your little neighborhood gang in Los Angeles could draw attention from Houston, Texas, Seattle, Washington, or Atlanta, Georgia.

Knowing your gang became a way to not only help yourself but also help cops on the other side of the country.

I was once flown up to Tacoma, Washington, on a federal drug case involving the "Bloodstone Villains," a neighborhood gang in Newton

Street Division. The case involved seven members of the gang who were claiming that they were thereby "coincidence," caught some drug cases and didn't know that each other from the same gang was also up there. They were trying to avoid the whole conspiracy aspect of the charges.

The FBI came to one of the local police stations to interview me and told me, "We hear you're the man as far as Bloodstone Villains is concerned."

They then showed me seven photos of gang members to see if I knew them, and I did all of them. One agent turned to his partner and said, "He's our man!"

A few months later, I was up in Tacoma, Washington testifying on those gang members on their federal drug case, and they were all convicted. Those agents and the prosecutor did a lot of work on that case to bring it to a successful conclusion. I did very little work, but due to my knowledge of those gang members, I held an important piece of that puzzle. My contribution helped to the success of that case.

I didn't learn the "Bloodstone Villains" so that I would be able to testify against them in a Tacoma, Washington courthouse. I learned them for my own everyday safety and for the everyday safety of the people living in Newton Street Division in south/central Los Angeles. My knowledge of that gang helped to prosecute several of them for spreading their criminal ways hundreds of miles away from Los Angeles.

I was kind of in hiding for a couple of days before I testified, but when it was my time, I walked into the courtroom, and I could see seven jaws drop. The defendants knew I knew all of them quite well. After I testified, I expected a barrage of questions from the seven defense attorneys … one for each of the gangsters. I only got one question, and that was from the attorney of a gangster who actually helped me to arrest a rape suspect. We were chasing a gang member who was wanted for rape. The suspect ran into an apartment in the hood, and we surrounded it and had him cornered.

The gang member in question walked up to the scene, and knowing it was his homeboy we had cornered in the apartment, I asked him to get his homie to come out before we called SWAT to respond to our location. He actually reasoned with the barricaded rape suspect and got him to come out and surrender.

The attorney asked me about that incident, and I explained what had happened. He was still found guilty like his homeboys.

To make my point even clearer, I once taught a class of LAPD officers, and I had one approach me after class. He was assigned to the 77th Street Division in south/central Los Angeles and shared a story with me.

A four-year-old black child was shot and killed on Halloween night a few years earlier. The little boy was wearing a Spiderman costume at the time, and I remembered the incident. It was another non-newsworthy event that had taken place in the inner city.

It was one of many that sadly happened on a regular basis.

This officer, who had nothing to do with the radio call, crime, arrest, or subsequent investigation, received a subpoena on the case. Apparently, a Crip gang member had been arrested on the case, and it was set to go to trial. The defendant was fighting the case and fighting the fact he was a gang member because it might influence the jury negatively and would add enhancements to his sentence during the penalty phase of the case.

This officer, who had nothing to do with the case or investigation, had written a field Interview card on this suspect a few months earlier during a contact in the field.

The officer identified him as a "Kitchen Crip" and knew him by his gang nickname, documenting it on the field interview card. Months later, the officer had to testify to those facts in a murder trial which he did.

The gang member was found guilty of killing the little 4-year-old boy dressed in his Spiderman outfit on Halloween night.

The officer was now beginning to tear up as he continued and said to me, "You know … I had nothing to do with the arrest or the case. I just wrote the field interview card and knew the guy. I think that might have been one of the most important things I've done while I've been on this job." He then told me that he just wanted to share that with me … and I was very glad that he did.

That officer will always remember the importance of that field interview card because I could see it in his eyes. He will also always remember the picture of that 4-year-old child in his Spiderman outfit because I could see it in his eyes … and it was also locked in his memory bank.

Your expertise is not what or how much you know but who you help to make better and how you make this a better world.

And by the way, make sure you always "know your backyard."

"Having a sense of duty."

February 28, 1997, is a date that will be etched in many people's minds, especially in the city of Los Angeles. It was the date of the infamous "North Hollywood Shootout," in which two heavily armed suspects attempted to rob the Bank of America Branch in North Hollywood.

During their subsequent escape attempt, an hour-long shootout occurred between the suspects and an "under-armed" contingent of courageous LAPD police officers. In all, twelve police officers and seven civilians were injured. Both suspects were killed.

When the shootout first started, I remember being in our office in downtown Los Angeles. Our gang unit shared a large third-floor office space with about 5 or 6 other non-related detective squads. Someone saw it on the TV set and called out to everyone who began to watch the whole scenario as it was playing out on the squad room television. I was there with a couple of members of our squad, and I told them, "Let's roll out there!"

I couldn't sit back and watch it going on like everyone else did. In their defense, I must say that this was an extremely unusual incident, and you'd think that by the time someone left downtown LA and got to North Hollywood, there'd be enough officers already there, and the situation would be under control. Well, it wasn't.

When we got there, it was chaos, and the situation was still unveiling. There was also a cordoned-off section a few blocks in size where civilians were not allowed to enter. I entered the location along with two very brave and loyal members of our squad, Wayne Caffey and Ed Hulbert. None of the three of us looked like cops, and we each had our own undercover police vehicle that did not look like a police vehicle.

Our strategy was to slowly drive up and down the streets of the "hot zone" within view of each other. Hopefully, one of the bank robbery suspects would approach one of us while attempting to carjack their way out of the area. While that was occurring, one of the other two of us (or both) would run him over with their police vehicle. Hey, desperate times call for desperate measures.

I recall slowly driving up and down those streets for about 20 minutes. It was pretty eerie because it was a beautiful sunny California day, and most everyone in this neighborhood was off the streets like a ghost town. At this time, no one knew how many suspects were actually involved, and it was still an unstable and non-secured crime scene.

Eventually, both of the suspects were shot and killed by the police while trying to escape that robbery. Wayne, Ed, and I never did encounter any of the suspects on that fateful day in North Hollywood. I admit that it was a scary situation cruising up and down those streets on that particular day, waiting for who knows what. The confidence that Wayne, Ed, and I had in each other, along with our experience and focus, helped to control our fear of the situation.

But what got us from downtown Los Angeles to North Hollywood was a sense of "duty." While many other fellow officers sat in disbelief, watching as the infamous "North Hollywood Bank Shootout" played out in front of a nation of onlookers, we hauled ass from downtown LA to the valley out of a "moral obligation" to our fellow officers, to the community and to ourselves. To us, at that moment, it was the "right thing" to do. It was our "duty."

The unfortunate thing about having a sense of duty is that most of the time, you never get enough credit for your obligation to your duty, and I'm not just talking about police work.

So, let's say that you don't get the accolades or praise you deserve for "doing the right thing" or for your personal sacrifices. Then what do you get?

You get a certain amount of self-satisfaction, and you can't put a price on that. Whether you are in the desert in Afghanistan, in a fifth-grade classroom in south/central Los Angeles, or reading a bedtime story to your child in Atlanta, Georgia, your sense of obligation to do what's right defines the person that you are. Your obligation to your family, to your neighbor, or to your fellow man might go unnoticed, but it says a lot about you, and that can never be minimized.

And although it seems like no one is noticing what you are doing, the most important person does, and that person is you. Unless you hear differently, you must assume that you are making a difference in people's lives, even if it's only one little life.

I really believe there's some higher being somewhere else keeping track of all of this.

"This is the law enforcement career ... mentally, physically, emotionally, and spiritually. Enjoy the ride." Whenever a young person asks me questions about a law enforcement career looking for advice, I tell them that it's a great job. But I also let them know to be ready to ride the ultimate roller coaster.

For me, the roller coaster lasted 32 years, not counting the work I have done in my post-LAPD career.

Mentally, emotionally, physically, and spiritually the highs can be remarkably high, and the lows can be terribly low. Some of those lows can last for years. I experienced a "low" that lasted three years and took a real toll on me.

One of the features that attracted me to law enforcement was the fact that it's such a difficult career; not just anybody can do it successfully. I'm also including the various aspects of law enforcement, such as probation, parole, corrections, prosecutors, and not just police officers. They all have their unique challenges, and again, not just anyone can do the job. I usually advise inquiring minds that highs are high and the lows are low, and most of all, it's a marathon and not like running a 100-yard dash. The qualities that will get you to the end of your career are endurance, resilience, and enthusiasm.

Endurance is the strength and fortitude to keep pushing forward. I have never been a long-distance runner, but in the police academy, running those hills in Elysian Park helps develop the mental endurance to push on even when you have nothing left in the gas tank. Trust in yourself so that you can push on.

Resiliency is the ability to recover and fight back whenever things go wrong. After a few bouts with adversity, you gain the self-confidence to know you will bounce back.

You're kind of like the "cockroach from hell." No matter how many times you get stepped on, once they lift their foot, you're off and running again.

Enthusiasm is the mental energy that pushes you day after day, year after year. Things like morale, working conditions, negativity, health, personal issues, and poor leadership can affect your enthusiasm; a lack of enthusiasm, endurance, and resilience leads to personal and professional suffering.

So, despite the normal challenges and obstacles life hands you, a law enforcement career will magnify them.

Knowing that, I hope you have a rewarding and mind-blowing career, and remember that the real daredevils raise their hands in the air when they are racing downhill.

That's the stuff you live to talk about.

Chapter 2 - Crime and the Community

***"If people didn't want the police, they wouldn't call ... and they keep on calling and calling ...."*- Tony "Pac-Man" Moreno.**

The greatest myth ... everybody hates the police

Since I came on the job in 1975, there has been an anti-police movement. In fact, before I came on the job, there was an anti-police movement. In the Los Angeles area, on the heels of the Watts Riots in 1965, the countless anti-war (anti-authority) demonstrations, and the East LA riots, the anti-police sentiment was visible.

This is actually one of the things that attracted me to a law enforcement career. Being society's "unpopular underdog" and how only a special kind of person could be successful at that job. Not just anybody could do it and do it well. Challenge accepted.

Nowadays, with social media and the mainstream media being what they are, the anti-police movement appears stronger and more widespread.

That's because controversial incidents like Michael Brown in Ferguson, Freddie Gray in Baltimore, Eric Garner in New York, Ezell Ford in Los Angeles, and so on are connected. In reality, one incident has nothing to do with the other, but the "movement" would have you believe that all of those incidents are tied together and evidence of widespread racism among law enforcement officers across the country. The mainstream media buys into this because "sizzle" (or, in this case, controversy) sells. People doing nice things and the world going smoothly are not interesting news items. The media instead is looking for that next controversial police incident to ride the momentum of that powerful anti-police horse.

Even though I am the first to admit that police misconduct does occur, and sometimes things do go wrong, it is not to the extent that the "movement" would have you believe. In regards to law enforcement itself, things are not as bad as the perception being created as an out-of-control, racist army. In reality, it's just not that way, and here are some reasons why.

First off, when a controversial incident does happen, the person involved with law enforcement is usually committing a crime or, at the very least, not complying with an officer's orders. They are out of compliance in a given situation, creating a confrontation.

Even if in each of these newsworthy, controversial incidents, the citizen involved was minding his or her own business and totally innocent of any misconduct (in most cases, it was an arrest situation), the number of those incidents is a minute fraction compared to the thousands of police/community contacts that happen on a daily basis. It's just not the widespread police brutality or misconduct that society is led to believe of today's law enforcement. If it were true, there would be thousands upon thousands of "Rodney King-type" videotapes floating around in the media and on the Internet.

There aren't.

The best evidence that most people do not hate the police is that on a daily basis, police departments across the country receive hundreds of thousands of calls for service. If the police were the true enemies of the people, nobody would ever call the police. People would handle their own situations in their own way.

In many communities, supporting the police may not be popular or fashionable, but trust me, most of the people in these neighborhoods call the police, depends on the police, and want the police.

If you don't believe this to be true, visit your local agency's communications division and listen to the calls roll in. Crime statistics around the country are initiated by someone in the community reaching out to law enforcement. And we're not counting the calls for service where no report was needed or generated.

It can be challenging and difficult for law enforcement but don't adopt a belief that everyone hates you. They don't. They may not be in a position to show their support, but they do need you and are probably amazed at how you are still able to do your job.

Remember, not everyone can do what you do. Meanwhile, those calls keep coming in.

"The best form of 'community engagement' is restoring public faith ... being effective."

I can tell you from working in a very busy area of Los Angeles in the late 70s and early 80's that I learned what "community engagement" actually meant ... and we didn't call it that back then.

Back then, you could drive down the street in a high crime area, and the kids might say hi to you, but they were normally reserved for the fact that they didn't want to appear too cozy with the cops. In many aspects, the cops were the outsiders to the neighborhood ... not a part of it.

How do you fix that?

You fix that by becoming an asset to the people of the community. You become an asset by making them safer and allowing them to live their lives in peace and harmony. There are 2 ways to do that:

1. You become a constant presence in the neighborhood, discouraging the negative elements in the community from implementing their will and taking control to their advantage, not the community.

2. You remove the criminals, gang members, and otherwise "negative influences" from that community. You are the true defenders of the community.

Only when you have both of those factors present and are consistently effective will you have 'true community engagement?' I can go to a 'coffee with a cop' or some similar event and take pictures to show the extent of the public cooperation that exists between the cops and the people.

But when it gets dark, I have to go inside my home, lock the doors, and hope we make it through another night that is not community engagement. It's great public relations and looks and sounds good, but does it change the living conditions of the residents?

Community engagement takes trust on both sides … the community and the police. It takes a relationship that goes beyond the surface of goodwill and humanitarianism. It has to be for more than the show or how it looks. It has to be a trust that exists when no one else is looking. People's lives might depend on that trust.

In the early 1980s in south/central Los Angeles, we had an explosion of "rock houses" that popped up out of nowhere. Their emergence coincided with the import and distribution of rock cocaine into and from Los Angeles. To me, "rock houses" were the ultimate joke on the people of the United States and especially those living in the "rock house" neighborhoods. This was also during the nation's "war on drugs."

The joke was that those evil criminals and gang members would set up shop in a place where kids had to walk past going to school every day. But I did notice that "rock houses" only sprung up in certain neighborhoods in south/central Los Angeles and nowhere else. Why was that?

Why weren't there "rock houses" in Eagle Rock, Van Nuys, Westchester, and other parts of the city?

They weren't tolerated in the other parts of the city. The criminals in the parts of the city where rock houses flourished felt that they had such a psychological hold on members of that community that this was a means of flexing their muscles … so to speak.

The criminals didn't care about the people of the community, the kids, the parents, the elderly, the disabled, and the working people; they didn't care. They were doing what they did to make money and don't get in their way.

That was an environment where the people really needed the police 24/7.

Don't judge "community engagement" by good public relations and photo shoots; judge it by the amount of trust the community has in the police and the extent to which the police are truly there for the community, 24/7.

"The more the people and officers communicate ... the safer the community."

I say this because I have worked in some very dangerous neighborhoods in Los Angeles, and although I may have thought this, I realized this was true in 2010 when I took a trip to Honduras.

I was with a close friend, Nelson Arriaga, who is a retired Sergeant from Inglewood (Ca.) Police Department and Executive Director of the California Gang Investigator's Association (CGIA). Nelson was born in Honduras and moved to Los Angeles when he was very young. He still has family in Honduras. We were in Honduras to do a gang assessment for the U.S. Government because of all of the "transnational" gang activity between the two countries.

We did a lot of interesting things during the week we were there. We spent most of our time in Tegucigalpa, which is the capital city of the country. We also spent time in San Pedro Sula, which at that time was considered the "most dangerous city in the world."

While we were there in Honduras, we visited a prison where many of the hardcore gang members are housed and where a week earlier, authorities recovered a cache of weapons from inside the prison.

We toured some of the substations and the neighborhoods they covered. Some of those places were "officer safety" nightmares due to the lighting, terrain, housing, and public access. I couldn't imagine working in neighborhoods like those with their challenges.

We were able to provide some training to officers and prosecutors and speak to officials regarding our experiences with our mutual interests, mainly the 18th Street and Mara Salvatrucha gangs. We saw plenty of their members down there, including a few who had been to Los Angeles and other parts of the U.S.

I remember being taken to a warehouse where "old cases" were stored. There were in excess of 5,000 murder cases there, and no one was ever going to investigate them unless a clue dropped in someone's lap. That was highly unlikely.

We were in San Pedro Sula on a Saturday afternoon when there was a shooting at a park. We were the second unit to get to the location, and it was a huge park full of people. It turns out that a group of men dressed as cops in dark clothing and masks over their faces pulled up in some black SUVs. They went to the soccer field, stopped the game, and gathered the players in a circle in the center of the field. They then began to shoot them with automatic weapons.

The suspects fled in their vehicles, and when all was said and done, 14 victims lay dead, most of them on the soccer field. Luckily for us, the suspects had left just prior to our arrival.

Although Nelson and I were very close friends and provided training together, we had never actually worked together in an emergency-type situation like this. We both responded very well due to our mutual training and were to organize the priorities of the scene itself, helping the Honduran authorities to establish and secure the crime scene and locate witnesses.

There were plenty of people in the park that day, so there were a lot of witnesses. When you've worked homicide or have been to a few crime scenes, you can tell by looking at people's faces who might have something to say to you, although this park, like many places in this part of the country, did not seem to encourage cooperation with law enforcement. Nobody was saying very much despite 14 people were lying there dead.

We had the local gang officer with us, and when I suggested to him that he might want to work the crowd to see if there were any witnesses that might want to share some info, he looked at me like I was crazy. He then said to me, "That's the job of the homicide detectives. We don't get involved in that. That's their job."

That was a very weird attitude to have, especially as a gang cop, because working with homicide detectives in Los Angeles, whenever there was a homicide with gang overtones, either victim or suspect, the detectives would expect you to have some info regarding the victim or suspect when they arrived at the crime scene.

They expected you to help them solve the case. That's where the pride in doing your job comes from "knowing your stuff."

I asked him what he was supposed to do, and he said basically, "Hang out" and see if they needed anything. What would they need … coffee and doughnuts?

"Don't forget the people you'll never meet."

I've repeated this story many times. It's about riding with a veteran officer when I was still pretty young. We were working the graveyard shift and driving through a pretty active neighborhood at about three in the morning. On this morning, it was real quiet, and all the lights of the houses were turned off. Everyone was sleeping.

My partner, all of a sudden, pulls our police car to the curb and parks. He then says to me, "You see all of these houses with the lights off? Don't forget the people that live in them. You may never meet them, but they depend on us.

That's why they can sleep at night.

My point is that although people always seem to be whining about the police, not everyone feels that way. Most people respect us; we just never hear about it.

Don't forget the people you'll never meet."

Thinking about the people you'll never meet can help keep you from sinking into a deep hole of negativity when you think about the public's view of law enforcement. It's easy to sink into that hole and let it affect you, your attitude, and your job.

The problem is that negativity can spill out onto the other important people in your life. People may care about you, but not many want to be around negativity for very long because it can suck away the life in a room.

In high-crime neighborhoods where it can seem as though the police are not the most popular people around, the citizens might support the police, but they can't do so out in the open, especially in gang-ravaged neighborhoods. You don't even know it, but you might be the only glimmer of hope that some people have to keep them feeling safe. It happens on a regular basis.

Whenever you begin to feel that society is stacked up against the police and there's no way you can do your job and make a difference, "Don't forget the people you'll never meet."

"If you expect police work ... you'd better condone police work."

A predominant perception in our 2022 society is that the public doesn't want an aggressive or proactive police force. In fact, the message to many of the "leaders" in law enforcement is that the activities and methods used by law enforcement officers must be curtailed and restrained. This becomes obvious when looking at some of the policies, training, and methods of operation adopted by some law enforcement agencies.

The truth is certain policies, training, and methods of operation are adopted in an effort to appease a loud, disgruntled portion of the public. It turns out that in many cases, that loud disgruntled voice of the public really only represents a small segment of society. By catering to the smaller vociferous groups, we are allowing that loud voice to dictate the manner in which law enforcement conducts itself on a daily basis. That is in contrast to the original concepts of law enforcement set forth by Sir Robert Peel, considered the "original Godfather of modern-day policing" back in 1829 in London, England. In his own words, Peel stated that law enforcement must not cater to public opinion and must provide service to all members of society.

So if a few members of the community, for whatever reason, want a softer, less aggressive approach to policing in their community, they win because they are the loudest voice. The larger silent majority segment of the community doesn't have a vote in the matter. They lose because their voice isn't heard or even considered in the matter.

Two things must occur to rectify this issue and ensure that law enforcement is providing service to all members of the community, not just catering to a select few.

First, when dealing with police/community relations, law enforcement leadership must do a better job of "taking the pulse" of the entire community. If you're going to do what's best for everybody, you need to know what's best for everybody. That means developing inroads so those silent voices are heard and considered when decisions are being made in regard to the welfare and safety of the entire community.

Second, if it takes a stronger, aggressive police force to make the community safe, the public must condone those methods of policing.

That doesn't mean condoning police brutality or misconduct. It does mean accepting the fact that sometimes police work can be an unpleasant thing to watch. It does mean having an understanding and empathy for what the job of enforcing the law entails. It means understanding that those sworn to uphold the law and protect society from the evil that exists must be allowed to be strong and supported in their mission to do so.

The more that a law enforcement officer feels supported and allowed to do his or her job, the better job they will do. It's human nature.

If someone is hanging around out in front of my residence at 3:00 am with no apparent purpose, I want an officer to stop and investigate and find out what that person is up to.

If it happens to be my teenage son, we will resolve his presence being there at that time. If it is someone with no logical purpose for being there, I want that officer to establish that fact and deal with it. That is what I expect.

I condone and appreciate that the officer is doing his or her job. That makes our community safer ... pretty simple.

"Most people suffer from' selective outrage'... they really care when it's convenient."

In Chapter #7 of the book I wrote, Cops in America ... Dealing with the Ferguson Effect ... "Forgotten Angels," you'll see the names of 53 children and young adults who have been victimized and killed by violent crime in recent years. They represent a cross-section of the country and share one common trait — none of them have gained national fame or are household names due to their particular incident. None of them deserved to die or were involved in any "suspicious" activity that led to their death. They were all innocent victims.

As I was researching information for that portion of the book, I came across so many violent crimes and young victims that I eventually had to stop listing them because those types of crimes just continue to occur. It doesn't stop.

In each case, I'm sure there was an amount of local outrage, especially among the family members, close friends, schoolmates, politicians, law enforcement, and the local residents. How could you not be outraged? Nobody deserves to bury his or her child, regardless of the circumstances.

Well, the children in Chapter #7 were not within a hundred miles of doing anything wrong. There was no controversy, no conflicting versions of what had happened. There was no rhyme or reason for most of it. They are just more examples of the vicious violence that continues to plague our streets and neighborhoods.

In Milwaukee, a three-year-old girl was shot and killed while she sat on her grandfather's lap.

In Kansas City, Kansas, a ten-year-old girl was watching the World Series on TV with her family when a car drove by, and the occupants fired numerous shots into the residence, killing the young girl.

In Brunswick, Georgia, a 13-month boy was being pushed in his stroller by his mother when she was approached by two gang members who demanded her money. When she didn't have money, they executed the baby boy in his stroller.

In those three cruel and brutal acts of violence, does anybody outside of their families or the area where they occurred to know the names of those three dead children? Probably not... and why not? Because they weren't killed at the hands of the police. And if they aren't killed at the hands of the police, it isn't newsworthy enough for the national media.

As I sat back and watched the outrage over the Ferguson situation grow day by day, it really began to outrage me. The reason I became so upset was that if the national conscience was going to step up and draw the line on human behavior, where have they been for these acts of violence when all of this pent-up outrage should have presented itself? Where were they for these kids?

If people are rising up in outrage over the specific violent confrontations in Ferguson, Baltimore, New York City, and Minneapolis, where the circumstances were controversial and in debate, why haven't they risen up in any of the following situations where there is no debate? The following cases are acts of sheer cold-blooded violence ... sheer evil. Yet none of these victims are household names on a national scale equal to those involved in those deadly confrontations with the police.

I'm not even debating what occurred in those police-involved situations that caused the national protests. Those are situations that will be forever disputed and argued about. I'm talking about instances where there is no debate ... no controversy ... no argument about who was right or who was wrong.

It's obvious to me that the primary issue isn't violence or even what is good for society as a whole. The issue is the anti-police sentiment. As you read this chapter, you'll discover that there is nothing else that really makes sense.

Even when you consider the #BlackLivesMatter theme, how come to those lives don't matter when it is black versus black violence, and the police are not involved? The majority of the following cases involved young, black, innocent victims. But there were no national protests, no national leaders showing up, and no celebrity or professional athletes showing their concern in a manner that created a significant national message.

My point is that in a lot of this anti-police, social concern rhetoric, there is great hypocrisy. As you read over some of the following scenarios, you'll scratch your head and wonder why there is so much "selective outrage" in this country.

I feel that if you have the time and energy to voice your outrage whenever the police are involved in a controversial act of violence, you should have the same concern for your fellow human being to step up and make yourself known when an act of violence is committed in a non-controversial, predatory and evil manner. If you can't do that, you may be a hypocrite and practicing "selective outrage."

Trust me, if you have a bone to pick with the police over a certain incident that may have occurred in your community, I can respect your concern and involvement as a citizen to protest and demonstrate. But if you don't have the same concern and passion over a senseless act of violence committed in your community by someone other than the police, your motives come into question.

The reason that some people are selective in their outrage is that the police make for an easy target. You can go on camera and criticize them. You can march in front of them and point your finger at them, and more than likely, nothing will happen to you. You can step up at a city hall meeting and be loud and disruptive to gain attention. The cameras, the crowds, and the atmosphere provide a certain amount of "comfort" to the antagonist. Even if a person were to get arrested or involved in a minor scuffle with the police, they then become a martyr. If they are lucky enough, they may even get a payday out of it by winning some type of lawsuit for being a "victim."

The truth is that if a 5-year-old child was to get shot and killed by the local gang, that same "concerned citizen" is not going to be found. They aren't going to go to the suspect's house and march in front of it in protest. They aren't going to display their disgust by holding a demonstration at the local park or apartment building where that gang hangs out. They're not going to go on the local TV news and verbally degrade the local gang that committed the murder.

Why does that citizen lose their concern and outrage when it is an innocent child cut down in senseless gang violence? Because gangs and gang members aren't easy targets to protest against. They don't play by the same rules that the police and the rest of society play by. They will retaliate against you for your "outrage."

When your life and welfare are at stake, it's not so easy to voice your outrage and demand change. The only people outraged by gang violence are the victims, the victim's families, friends, and other relatives, politicians, and the true warriors of the neighborhood, the people who are fed up with it.

I saw a photo of a group of people marching to rally for peace in Kinston, North Carolina. There were about 35-40 people in all, and they had been experiencing a rise in violent crime. Why weren't there more people marching? Because there was no national attention, it's not a trendy topic, and you're liable to get on the wrong side of the gang members in that area. In this case, it's safer not to be outraged and mind your own business.

The national media doesn't care because it's not sexy or provocative enough to be newsworthy. It's just the people in Kinston victimizing each other. It's like the people in Newark or Los Angeles, or Baltimore. You might get their attention if you have a large amount of violence within a short period of time, like 12 shootings in two days. But then, the number of shootings is the story. Who got shot and why they got shot doesn't matter. The national media expects violence in the community and is not intrigued by it.

And do you know why the national media doesn't care? Because as members of society, we don't care unless it involves the police, is race-related, and/or is controversial. That is what makes money.

"Everyone wants the truth, but no one wants to be honest." – Unknown.

"No matter how pretty a picture we paint, someone still has to wrestle the alligators."

Part of the law enforcement image nowadays is the kinder and softer police force. It really doesn't matter if crime is going up and everyone, including the police, are victims.

So as police departments across the board strive to give the impression that they are kinder and gentler, they are hiding the fact that enforcing laws can sometimes be an ugly, dirty job. I understand all about image and public relations, but I also understand that when we in law enforcement are not truthful about the enormous responsibilities involved with that job, we can lose public trust.

Part of the problem is that there are those in law enforcement who don't present an honest view of what the job entails. There is honor, respect, kindness, and empathy that come with the territory.

But there is also the dark side of the law enforcement world. There is the violence, the evil people, the victimization, and the unfairness of it all.

People don't really want to see the ugliness of our jobs. They just expect us to do it the right way their way, whatever that might be. They also do not want to see the difficulties in the job. Anything that comes our way is met with, "Well, you asked for the job."

I may have asked for the job, but I didn't particularly ask for the situation.

We want to be fair, honest, and trustworthy, but we skirt around the idea of being "down and dirty" with the criminals who prey on the public. If I lived in a crime-ridden neighborhood where it was unsafe to be out at night, I wouldn't appreciate having "coffee with a cop" if they weren't around when I really needed them. If they weren't there to disrupt or discourage the daily criminal ways of gang members or other criminals, then to me, they aren't doing their job. It doesn't matter what color the skin of the evil-doer is. Evil is evil, and wrong is wrong. People care about their safety and the safety of their loved ones.

Law enforcement leadership tends to forget about the people locked behind their doors at night, too afraid to run to the market or simply enjoy sitting on their own porches. If we don't think about them, they don't exist.

That's the same as a crime not reported, a crime that never existed. When we say crime is up, we actually mean only reported crime is up … not actual crime. Think about that. Think about if we were able to record every actual crime. Think how high the crime rate would be then.

In reality, we need officers who understand how difficult the job of being "society's protectors" is and who relish the thought of being that type of "hero." That is what has always made law enforcement an honorable profession and a challenging one.

When I talk to a young person about a career in law enforcement, I try to assess how well the person will do in those moments or if they even acknowledge that those moments exist.

Those times when no matter how things might look, you are strong enough to stand behind your thoughts, decisions, and your word. You stand up in the face of the storm.

Most people have never been tested to that point.

Those are the times I call "wrestling with the alligators," and the potential for those times is always there. But because those times are usually unpleasant or uncomfortable, we in law enforcement don't prepare for or even acknowledge them. "Don't look ... maybe it will go away."

I believe that any young person that is thinking about law enforcement as a career choice had better bare in mind that no matter how much pomp and circumstance, decorum, dignity, and respect come with the job, the candidate had better be ready to wrestle the alligators.

That means that no matter what you look like, how big or small you are, what color your skin is, whether you're a man or woman, how old you are, or your political position, when the time comes to "get dirty," you "get dirty."

When you expect trouble, you handle it better. If you try to ignore trouble, sometimes it finds you. When trouble finds you, you had better be ready for it. I have always tried to be in the frame of mind that I was "looking for trouble,"... not looking to "make trouble." There's a difference, and that becomes more obvious with experience.

Just remember that no matter how your agency preserves its image and presents a kinder, softer department, someone will always have to "wrestle the alligators." That's the 500-pound elephant in the room because no one wants to talk about it because it doesn't fulfill the "image" of law enforcement. But it is why you accepted the difficult job.

Take it from me. If you decide on a law enforcement career, good for you. If you get into this career with the hope of a good-paying job, good benefits, and a good retirement, you will deserve all of it.

But listen to me when I say someone still has to "wrestle the alligators." Those people wrestling those alligators are on the frontline, so I hope you enjoy that part of it, especially when you are new to it.

But when you take the law enforcement job, you go "all in." Going "all in" means taking the good with the bad, the magic moments with the "shit on your hands" moments.

Those are the times I call "wrestling with the alligators," and the potential for those times is always there. But because those times are usually unpleasant or uncomfortable, we, in law enforcement, don't prepare for or even acknowledge them. "Don't look; maybe it will go away."

And if you really do like wrestling the alligators, you will be invaluable to your agency or department. And like anything else you enjoy in life, your passion will make you very, very good at it.

That would be something you can be very proud of.

Chapter 3 – Kids and Family

"I have a dream that my four little children will one day live in a nation where they will not be judged by the color of their skin but by the content of their character."
– Dr. Martin Luther King, Jr.

"Unfortunately, it's easier to give a kid excuses than to develop his character. That is the lazy person's way of parenting."

Parenting is the hardest job in the world, even with two involved and caring parents. Unfortunately, that's not the makeup of the "average" American family. The traditional family structure has taken a real beating over the years.

Many of the communities experiencing high crime rates, gang activity, and persistent violence contain a family unit and leadership within the home, which are overburdened and sometimes almost non-existent.

Leadership within the home, regardless if the "leader" is a mom, dad, grandmother, grandfather, older sibling, other relative, or family friend, is vital. A child needs to learn what responsibility is, how to respect others, be a productive part of society, and how to function and grow within the rules and laws of society.

Even with a stable family unit in place, in many low-income and minority communities, a child still needs outside support to grow up and become responsible; support people like teachers, coaches, relatives, clergy, friends, and other role models, which may include a law enforcement officer, are invaluable. Most politicians and law enforcement leaders won't tell you that for fear of being labeled a "racist."

Politicians and leaders are letting society down by playing into the excuse game, encouraging people, especially kids, young adults, and their parents, to use excuses to explain and justify bad behavior.

There are no consequences for that behavior, and if there are, the excuses tend to promote leniency and avoidance of personal responsibility.

Excuses are killing society, and many substandard parents use those excuses because it's convenient and lets them "off the hook" for being responsible for their child. If the parents and family members use excuses to explain bad behavior, then that is what the child learns to avoid any personal responsibility.

Dr. Marin Luther King related he hoped that one day his children would be judged by society for the "content of their character and not the color of their skin."

If people were raising their children with the same concern that Dr. King emphasized, "content of character," this would be a much different world.

"What good families do"

1. **Good Families Provide Support**– which includes comfort, warmth, and reassurance. They band together during tough times and appreciate each other during the good times. Each of these experiences can help to bond family members together even more.

   One of the important areas of support is in education. Families should make a concerted effort to become involved in a child's education. Involvement is a great example of true support and shows a commitment to learning.

2. **Good Families Provide Vital Resources–** The family makes available food, shelter, money, transportation, and clothing. These resources create a stable environment that can enhance the ability of family members to concentrate and succeed in other areas of life.

While making a child comfortable, the family can also teach him to appreciate possessions, money, food, and clothing. They should make the child comfortable but also teach him not to take things for granted.

3. **Good families develop vital skills** - Skills development is an important function of parenting and family life. Children develop their physical, emotional, social, and educational skills by what they see. These skills are important because they make up the core or internal workings of the child that prepares them for adulthood.

The focus should be on developing positive self-esteem, a positive view of his environment, and a solid sense of purpose. He should also learn conflict resolution and self-control and adopt a non-violent attitude.

4. **Good Families Reinforce A Strong Family System** – Good families set the example of a strong family structure by displaying positive examples of leadership skills, decision-making, financial responsibility, and establishing appropriate roles within the family. A strong family system also includes administering discipline and establishing behavior standards.

Establishing roles also help the members learn about responsibility.

The family system can help the child accept responsibility, develop integrity, learn to care for family members and others, meet expectations and learn honesty.

"Advice on Kids and Young Adults"

- Make a clear distinction between right and wrong. The line between right and wrong doesn't normally change. Don't change it for their benefit.

- Don't let them expect the benefit of the doubt. If you always give them the benefit of the doubt, they will grow up looking for an excuse or an "out" during tough situations or decisions.

- Don't be a hypocrite. Don't say one thing and do another. You lose credibility with the child, and you'll get it thrown back in your face.

- Be the parent, not the best buddy. Your child will acquire friends. You need to be the one who sets boundaries and expectations and holds them with discipline. When they grow older and have their own kids, they will love you for it.

- Don't make excuses for them. When you make excuses and allowances for them, you risk creating a monster. When they fail or make a mistake, it doesn't reflect on you as a parent. It tests you, be ready.

- Being strong and consistent makes them better adults. Children learn more from what they see than what you tell them. Being strong and consistent with integrity is the best model they can have.

- Teach respect for authority. Don't let them grow up thinking that they don't have to adhere to rules, laws, and authority figures if they don't want to. Nobody is privileged, and allowing them to develop that negative attitude will hurt them in the future.

- Teach them to stand on their own two feet. Let them grow up developing their own individual strength and independence. The less they need to depend on anyone or anything, the better off they are.

- Let them fall and get up on their own. That's how they learn to conquer their fears and insecurities, by handling stress and pressure themselves. That's why I love youth sports. Kids don't need to be great athletes to get value from the experience.

- Don't allow violence or criminal behavior in the home. Kids learn more from what they see than what you tell them. Don't risk their future.

- Don't give gangs a chance. The gang offers a substitute for what the family and society fail to provide. It gives the child an escape from what they don't want to be or how they don't want to live.

"Break the Child Out of The Bubble."

I was born and raised in East Los Angeles, California. Back then, there was a very strong gang presence in the neighborhood, which was made up of probably 85-90% Hispanic population. For the most part, it was a lower to middle-income area, but I was a very happy child, not focusing on what we didn't have and appreciating what we did have.

I only had one other sibling, an older sister, and my dad spent a lot of time with me. He always told me that I could be whatever I wanted to be when I grew up … as long as I could read, spell, and write. So starting when I was 5-6 years old, he would bring home football and baseball cards, open the pack and announce the players that were in the pack. If I could spell the player's name, I could keep the card. If I couldn't spell the name, the card would go back into a pile that I could try to spell again at a later time.

It didn't take long for me to build up my card collection, but more importantly, I learned to read, write and spell. Those three qualities have helped me throughout my life and career.

My dad knew if I was to make something of myself and not be confined to living my life in a substandard lifestyle, I had to possess the qualities that would lift me out of that stereotypical lifestyle. I had to be able to break out of the bubble that our society sometimes locks kids and young adults into.

If you don't have high expectations for children and then surround them with excuses for failure, you might be determining their destiny. If you expect a kid to use drugs, drop out of school, or join a gang, that's what they will probably do. If you provide them with excuses to accept the negative behavior, it makes a stronger case for them to follow that particular path.

It is up to parents, teachers, coaches, relatives, concerned citizens, and the rest of us to help break those kids out of the "pre-destined bubble" some of those kids are living in.

But that takes work, and the truth is, a lot of people are lazy or preoccupied. They would rather raise a child with excuses and allow that child to live in a "limited world," never striving to reach out and experience a life that could be.

Society doesn't allow us to criticize a person's parenting … that's too personal. So to be politically correct, we avoid the heart of the problem and focus more on what to do when that child is in trouble. And once he or she is in trouble, we point at the "system" or the "environment" as the cause. We don't dare point at parenting.

On June 5, 2003, the Mighty Ducks of Anaheim lost Game Five of the Stanley Cup Hockey Finals 6-3 to the New Jersey Devils. I was at that game as a "guest" of Colonel Rick Fuentes, newly appointed Superintendent of the New Jersey State Police, and New Jersey Governor James McGreevy in the Governor's Luxury Suite. Watching a Stanley Cup Finals game in the luxury box with the governor himself; is not bad for a Latino kid who was born and raised in East Los Angeles and taught how to read using football and baseball cards.

I know how important it is for a kid to break out of the "bubble" because there shouldn't be a "bubble" in the first place … but there is and maybe always will be.

Learning how to spell the names from football and baseball cards got me a seat in the Governor of New Jersey's luxury box at a

Stanley Cup Finals hockey game. How many little Latino boys born and raised in East LA can say that?

Too bad Dad isn't alive to see this …

"Little Victories Count ...."

My father started to teach me how to read when I was about five years old. He would bring home baseball cards and ask me how to spell the player's name on the card, and if I could, I got to keep the card.

After a while, I had a nice collection of baseball cards, and I could spell everyone's name on them. To me, each card in my collection was an accomplishment. Each card was a small trophy or victory for me.

He also instilled in me confidence in my ability to read, write and spell. I knew that I was better than most of the kids around me.

What this also did was help me create a positive self-image and made me feel very good about myself as I grew up.

Most kids nowadays are products of their environment.

This means that they are affected and influenced by their surroundings and the people who are close to them and come into contact with them. Little victories are vital.

If you wonder why little kids bring home their test scores, drawings, and other little projects, it's because they are important to them. It is important for them to receive your praise and approval. Your praise and approval are building blocks that create their wall of self-confidence and make them feel like they are important.

Now, you shouldn't just throw praise around because sometimes kids can perceive that you are "just being nice" and don't really mean what you say.

I was recently at a little league game for 9 and 10-year-olds, and the score was 12-0. A mother from the team that was losing was trying to be positive and yelled out, "Keep it going, boys. You guys are doing great!"

One of the kids on the losing team turned to his teammate and said, "What is she smoking?"

So, that kid discounted that mother's well-intentioned "praise" because he felt that it was inappropriate and that she was just being nice. Kids can be very perceptive.

So, if you are a parent, teacher, older brother or sister, family member, coach, counselor, caretaker, school administrator, law enforcement officer, neighbor, community member, or any other person who has regular contact with kids, remember what you say to them does matter.

Remember that every little gold star, sticker, certificate, good grade, extra credit, trophy, and positive note counts. Give them a reason to celebrate themselves. They are all building blocks on that kid's wall of life.

Having a positive self-image doesn't guarantee that the child won't experience rejection. Rejection is just part of this competitive life that we all live.

Kids need to learn how to handle adversity. It's not always about winning because nobody always wins.

But feeling good about himself or herself will allow that kid to rebound and come back a better, stronger person.

And that's a lesson that applies to all of us.

"Teach Your Child 'Respect' And 'Compliance.' It Can Prevent Chaos Later in Life."

"If the police stop you, just do what they tell you and don't do anything stupid. If you do something stupid, I can't help you." – My Dad.

If you are a parent and you are concerned about raising a child in today's progressive world, let me give you some advice ... the same advice my dad gave me. Teach your child how to treat others.

I know growing up in East LA and dealing with the L.A. County Sheriff Deputies when I was a teenager saved me. It saved me when I was in situations when things could have gone really wrong, and I wouldn't have had any recourse other than to be a victim of the circumstances.

I think what saved me was the respect I showed the deputy, although I wasn't really wrong. I sensed that wasn't the time to debate "right or wrong" and just be lucky to walk away in "one piece."

When I was in high school, I got in my friend's car, and we went down to cruise Whittier Blvd. By the way, it was Halloween, and we had some eggs to toss at people .... all in good fun, of course.

We got pulled over by two deputies, and they got us out of the car we were in. We knew we had eggs and just tried to play it off as if we had bought some eggs for my friend's mom.

As they were talking to us, there was no tension, and we thought the dialogue went pretty well.

No one was drinking, and there were no weapons in the car because, trust me, they checked.

One of the deputies said to us, "OK, guys, you can leave. Just be careful out here; there's a lot of idiots out tonight." They waved at us as they left.

When we got in the car, we realized that they had smashed the eggs all over the back seat of my friend's car. It was a real mess, but what were we going to do? They knew why we had the eggs, and we knew why we had the eggs. My friend was a good guy, and although it was his car, we knew we got what we deserved. As longtime L.A. Lakers announcer, Chick Hearn would have said, "No harm, no foul."

A few weeks later, I was in another friend's car, and we got pulled over about a block from my house.

Again, it was by L.A. County Sheriff's deputies, different ones. They got us out of the car, and one of them walked over to me and said, "Do you remember me?"

Not to be smartass, but I didn't know what he was talking about. I said, "No."

He said, "You don't remember me chasing you into Eastmont Junior High School last night, and you got away?"

I said, "That wasn't me."

He asked me where I lived, and I told him … 10 houses away from Eastmont Junior High School.

Then he started to poke me in the chest with his right index finger, and he said, "You're lucky I didn't catch you last night. That would have been ugly, you little punk."

I was both scared and pissed off, but I held my tongue to not make matters worse. They did let us go, but my feathers were ruffled. I hadn't done anything and got a finger-poke scolding for my trouble.

I got home, and I was still a little pissed off, and my dad noticed. He asked me if everything was fine, and so I told him about our little talk with the deputies, finger poking and all. My dad believed me because I wasn't one to get in trouble. I was smart enough to avoid trouble.

My dad asked me what I wanted to do, and I told him, "Nothing."

He said, "We can go down to the sheriff's station if you want to …."

I decided against it.

I didn't want to waste my time or my dad's time.

"That's what I mean.

Even if you didn't do anything wrong, don't make things worse by acting like an ass. You did the right thing. It may not feel like it, but you did the right thing."

My dad had equipped me with the tools and knowledge of what to do if and when I ever was to get stopped by the cops. He didn't lecture me on how unfair things were and that if I were to get stopped by the cops and I hadn't done anything wrong, protest and don't cooperate. That would have made matters worse.

He taught me to have respect for law enforcement officers and comply with their instructions or orders.

If things don't go well and their instructions are questionable, that is not the time to protest. When the situation is diffused or is over, there will be time to review the circumstances and hopefully get things right.

My analogy comes from when I used to live across the street from the beach, and people would walk their dogs all of the time. A 110-pound woman is walking a big dog on a leash that she cannot control. If I am walking in the other direction on the same side of the street and I see her and the dog, I may just decide to cross the street and avoid her and her dog ... avoid the situation. It's not fair that I have to cross the street when I am out for a nice walk because she can't handle the big dog, but it is smart and prudent of me to do so. It is better in the long run.

It is my "situational awareness." Teach your child situational awareness and that sometimes things aren't fair. You want your child to make it through the situation with the least amount of chaos possible.

To me, that is you giving your child some practical, usable information. Avoid the chaos ... teach your child "respect" and "compliance."

"Truancy ... the biggest red flag."

Years ago, I read a study that said the average reading level for an inmate entering a state prison in California for the first time was 8th grade. The study also stated that once in prison, the reading level improved. This brought me to a couple of conclusions.

First, the results of the study made sense because kids having trouble in school usually begin to lose interest in middle school grades 6 through 8. In the 8th grade, unless they are motivated and attending class, that reading level probably isn't going to rise significantly.

Once in prison and attending class and reading on their own, reading improves. That shows the inmate was capable of learning and reading at a higher level all along. He or she just wasn't interested enough at the time.

Those middle school years are critical, with multiple classes and multiple teachers for the first time. The student has the responsibility of preparing for and getting to class. They get more homework than in elementary school, and they have to adjust socially with the stakes a bit higher. It's an adjustment for some kids, and if there is no support in the home or anywhere else outside the classroom, they could be destined to fail.

Evidence of this "collapse" and loss of interest is truancy.

It's one thing to struggle and get poor grades because a student can always get help. Failing to attend class demonstrates the student doesn't care ... or care enough.

I was on a board for the school district that would interview students with "chronic" truancy issues with their parents present. Many parents made excuses for the child, blaming the teachers, the school, the class, and the environment. But those parents weren't facing the real problem.

The child was losing interest, and in most cases, they needed help to re-engage and renew their interest in attending class.

Parents would also minimize the act of their child "ditching class" by saying things like, "Well, at least he's not doing really bad things like dealing drugs and running with gangs."

Those are the kind of parents who, years later, will be saying, "Well, he only robbed the 99 cents store. It's not like he robbed a bank or something."

If you know of a kid who is ditching class and not attending school, try to get them some help or at least let the parents know. Also, let them know that truancy is a cry for help and a warning of potentially bad things ahead for that child.

That's what a "red flag" is…

"The system doesn't put people in jail … choices do."
When I hear cries about the criminal justice system being systematically racist, I cringe. I cringe because so many people believe that or take it as fact, and what they are doing is making excuses.

There is no big political machine out scooping up black or brown people and putting them in prison.

But if I am black, brown, or the product of a lower-income environment, I can use that as my excuse and not have to worry about putting in the hard work that parenting requires. Racism is the excuse. The deck is stacked against you, and there's nothing you can do about it.

The only problem with that excuse is how do you account for the majority of black or brown people whose kids grow up to be productive adults? You can't.

Parenting is hard work, probably the hardest job in the world. People aren't signing up for that while they are having sex. Most people aren't thinking about that, but sometimes parenting comes with the territory.

When I was a teenager growing up in East Los Angeles, my dad would tell me to be respectful when dealing with law enforcement. My dad never expected me to be near or around any trouble, but he wanted me to be prepared if it ever happened in the case, and it did.

He also told me that if I ever acted like a smartass or did something stupid to a cop, he couldn't help me. He was right, and it probably saved my ass a couple of times. I wasn't out doing the wrong things, but I was around when other people were. That's the life of a teenager.

One of the things that a quality parent does is to help prepare a child for the decisions he or she will have to make later in life. If you aren't helping a child do that, you're not much of a parent.

It's a classic case of a child not doing well in school, so the parents have a meeting with the teacher.

In the "old days," the parents would learn what areas the child should or could improve on, and usually, the problem got corrected. As time has marched on and the traditional family structure has diminished, the parent/teacher meeting now takes place, and the parent now defends the child.

The child is not held accountable, and if that's what he learns, that is what the child will become, a person with excuses.

In the second scenario, the parent is not defending their child. They are really defending their own parenting skills or lack thereof. They are just making excuses.

The problem is as that kid becomes a young adult, excuses have little or no value. Excuses have no value because people know they are used to avoid responsibility. An excuse can justify failure, and as a parent, there may be reasons for substandard parenting, but there is never an excuse for it. The ease with which a parent makes excuses for a child's behavior is a window into the soul of that parent.

The problem is that criminals seem to get younger and younger when in reality, parenting is getting worse and worse.

Criminals nowadays can be found as young as 9, 10, and 11 years of age, and when they are that young, the trend seems to be non-punitive. Heck, the trend nowadays for criminals 16, 17, and 18 years of age is non-punitive, so how can we expect these young adults to make the right decisions when they have never been taught the "right decisions"? When it comes to making a decision, they have no qualms about doing wrong or making a bad decision.

When this happens enough, that individual develops a lack of empathy or conscience.

We have a society of people walking around with empathy and regard for their fellow man, and others never taught what having a conscience means. They act on impulse and not with empathy. To me, that goes back to a lack of parenting.

In many ways, the skill of parenting is on the decline, and for some, it's embarrassing to be called out for that weakness. Society just looks at all of the other causes of crime, and we collectively continue to go "down the tubes" as a nation.

I say that we should focus on the fact that not everyone is prepared or responsible enough to be a quality parent, and that is where our resources need to be placed. It may take a few years, but the difference would be noticeable.

The topic of "bad parenting" is the same as the "gang problem." If you ignore it, it doesn't go away; it gets worse. It is getting worse child by child, decade by decade, and generation by generation.

We need to break that cycle ...

"Dirty Little Hands"

In 2004, I had the opportunity to travel to Chiapas, Mexico, in order to represent the Los Angeles Police Department and participate in a Gang/Community Involvement Symposium involving dignitaries from the United States, Mexico, and various Central American countries. I had the honor of being the only law enforcement officer from the United States in attendance.

On one of the days, we had some free time, so many of us traveled to one of the smaller communities to do some sightseeing and get in some shopping. We were warned about catering to some of the local people who might try to "scam" us out of our money by begging and drawing on our sense of compassion due to their economic plight. We were also warned that giving in might begin an onslaught of other locals who would mob us after seeing that "free money" was being given away by us, the unsuspecting tourists.

It was pretty warm, and during one break, I snuck off away from our group to a little store in order to buy some juice. As I was in the store looking in the fridge where the cold drinks were kept, I felt someone or something pulling on my right pant leg at the knee. When I looked down, I saw a small, dark-haired, dark-skinned little boy about six years of age staring up at me. His face was pretty dirty, and his clothes were disheveled.

He said to me, "Senor, quiero jugo". He was telling me in Spanish that he would like some juice since that is what I was grabbing for myself.

I thought that maybe this was a ploy to get some money out of me and that he would summon the rest of his buddies and friends once he knew I was giving away free cash. I decided to test him, and I offered him some money instead.

"Quiere dinero? Cuanto dinero quiere?" I asked him.

To my amazement, he declined the free money offer and once again stated, "Quiero jugo, senor."

I again offered money, and again he declined.

A bit stunned, I figured that I would buy him the juice because now I believed that he was indeed thirsty. I asked what kind of juice he wanted, and he then stated, "Y puede comprar uno pa' mi amigo tambien?" He was asking in Spanish if I could also buy some juice for his friend, who was smaller and dirtier than him and now standing alongside me, staring up at my confused facial expression.

I gave in and let each of them pick their flavor of juice. As I paid for the three bottles of juice, the guy behind the counter took my money and acted as if they had just witnessed a drug deal go down and wanted no part of what was happening. As I gave them their bottles of juice and we headed for the front door of the store, a small part of me was still convinced that I had somehow been "taken," and I really expected to be mobbed by a flood of kids once I got out to the street.

For my own investigative satisfaction, I stopped the older boy before we exited the store and asked him, "Why don't you want money?"

In Spanish, he replied, "If you give me money, once we get out there, someone bigger will just take it from me. When you give me juice, once I drink it, it's mine."

We exited the store, and we went our separate ways. I was not mobbed by anyone and felt pretty bad because I had mistrusted these two little boys who were only thirsty and relying upon their survival skills to get by. I saw them walk off to my left and, due to my guilt, did not want to look back at them.

Ten minutes passed, and the group I was with was moving toward the transportation bus to go back to the hotel. Now almost a half block away from the store, I happened to glance back towards the store and saw the two little boys huddled together in an alcove, nursing and still enjoying their juice. They were looking down the street in my direction, and they both waved with their dirty little hands in a friendly gesture to me. I waved back, and someone in my group asked, "Who are you waving at?" because you couldn't really see the two boys unless you were looking for them.

I muttered, "Aw, just someone." I was so moved that I couldn't even talk.

When we left, I was speechless in thought for the entire two-hour bus ride back to the hotel.

It was one of life's moments that nails you right between the eyes. I really felt for those two little boys and their living conditions.

I hope that as you read this chapter, you can take some energy and motivation from it and continue on in your life's journey for the good of others, for the good of kids and young adults everywhere.

If you happen to wonder why we work, struggle, and endure to do what we do for our kids. If you wonder where the reward is, just look real hard. If you're lucky like I was on that day in Chiapas, Mexico, you'll see dirty little hands waving at you, too.

The motivation in what you do and in how you live your life then becomes very clear... and your experiences help make you who you are.

"The birthday cake" – excerpt from chapter #4 kids (spinach for the everyday warrior)

I once interviewed a real hardcore gang member that had spent over 30 years of his 50-year life in one correctional facility or another. I asked him if anything could have stopped him from taking the course in life that he did. He then told me an amazing story.

When he was in the sixth grade, he was summoned to the principal's office. When he got there, he was told by the secretary to have a seat and that the principal would be with him in a couple of minutes. While he sat and waited, he went over in his mind a handful of things that he might be in trouble for.

About then, the principal came out and called him into her office. The secretary followed them into the office. When he walked into the office, he saw that the vice-principal and the school nurse were also in her office, along with a birthday cake bearing his name and twelve lit candles. As he continued telling me this story, his eyes began to water, and he was holding back tears.

The group then sang "Happy Birthday" to him, and he blew out the candles. Tears are now flowing down his face as he continues talking to me. He said, "You know, that's the only time in my life that anyone ever sang "Happy Birthday" to me or gave me a birthday cake."

He then looked me square in the face and said, "A couple of more birthday cakes, and I wouldn't have turned out this way."

That was an excerpt from my second book, "Spinach for the Everyday Warrior."

What is equally amazing about that story is that the interview took place in a park, and the moment that was totally spontaneous was actually caught on videotape. I was working with a Canadian film crew that was trying to put together a documentary on street gangs in North America. They approached me about helping with a segment on L.A. gangs and agreed with my conditions. I told them not to expect me to be a clown-like character like the ones that punctuate the reality T.V. landscape. I wasn't going to be anyone's clown or have a gimmick. Secondly, I wasn't going to glamorize or glorify the violence. I envisioned a documentary that could have some depth and pertinence in order to give a better understanding of the gang problem. I could see a documentary that portrays the human side of the gang issue and the gray portions of it because not everything in the gang world is black and white. I hoped for a video that a parent could sit and watch with their child or a teacher could watch with her class and encourage discussion. Silly me ...

I thought that having a 50-year-old lifetime gang member pours his heart out on film would make for great T.V. I thought that his passion, regret, and words would make some youngster somewhere think about what he or she was doing with their life. Apparently, they wanted blood, violence, and misery. They wanted what is known as "sizzle" in the business. I refused to escort them into that part of their life, and they eventually moved on to Windsor, Ontario, due to a rash of violence that was occurring there. Hopefully, for them, it was gang violence.

I never heard from them again, and I don't believe that interview was ever aired. I would love to get my hands on it, though.

That interview was truly priceless.

Pac-Man Life

Tony Moreno

I never heard from them again, and I don't believe that interview was ever aired. I would love to get my hands on it, though.

That interview was truly priceless.

78

Chapter 4 – Leadership
"Leaders eat last." - Simon Sinek

"Talking About Leadership ..."

While involving myself with the gang problem my entire career, since 1982, I have traveled around North America and Central America, conducting training for thousands and thousands of law enforcement professionals.

I have also been able to meet and speak with a lifetime of dedicated people regarding their careers and their challenges. The one topic that continually pops up in conversation is "leadership." It is an especially sensitive issue when it comes to entry-level or frontline supervision.

It seems that the consensus throughout law enforcement is that the wrong people seem to get promoted and for the wrong reasons. This occurs because law enforcement is on a continual push to professionalize itself and enhance a polished image. This means an emphasis on "formal education" when assessing candidates for promotion, especially in supervisory and authority positions. Many agencies nowadays have a minimum amount of formal education in order to promote.

I'm not down on formal education, but law enforcement is a unique career with many unique jobs, tasks, and assignments. When you're dealing with people, common sense, instinct, and communication skills are vital. These traits are not emphasized when searching for the ideal person to promote.

In the eyes of many, formal education mixed with a lack of disciplinary issues makes for the perfect candidate.

In other words, if I can enter the world of policing with a college degree and stay away from conflict, critical situations, and controversy, I can promote it too. That's not really the mark of a leader or person that others look to during critical situations. That's the real mark of a good candidate or actually a "good student."

As I talk to more and more people about this issue, I have come to realize that this occurs outside of law enforcement as well. It's the candidate that walks into a job interview and looks great on paper. Once they open their mouth and begin to express their reasoning and critical thinking skills, you start to wonder what's wrong with the formal education process nowadays.

Instead of discussing the concepts of leadership and leaving it open to interpretation as to whether someone is a leader or not, I thought I'd make it easy for you, the reader. This book examines certain traits and behaviors that, when present, are evidence of poor leadership or a lack of leadership. Almost like rank or title, these traits are easily identifiable and hard to ignore. If you see some of these traits in yourself, maybe you should reevaluate your performance and effectiveness as a leader. If you are striving for promotion or anticipate being in a position of responsibility, being aware of these issues can maybe help you to become a better leader.

One of the problems I encountered while talking to people about leadership was that everyone, I mean everyone had their share of horror stories. As the conversations went on, I found myself discovering more types and examples of bad leaders. I originally tried to make it easy on myself by giving the bad leader in each chapter a nickname or moniker and using it as the chapter title, but I started to run out of names. Six chapters quickly grew to fifteen, and I had to stop somewhere, or I could have written a book that would have been larger than James Michener's Hawaii.

It was much simpler for me to identify the qualities that are "pro-leadership" because of the true leaders I have been exposed to.

When you are a leader, you don't have to go around telling people that you are a leader; you just are. The best leaders I have seen don't do it for image or accolades. They do it for the sake of others and usually at their own risk and sacrifice. That's what defines true leadership on the job and true leadership outside the job.

A friend once contacted me and told me that he had been through a certain, very prestigious "leadership school," and in that school, they highly discouraged their instructors from telling "war stories."

He knew he'd get my goat, and it did.

If you have "great leaders" as instructors and they are not allowed to use "war stories" in their training, what do they teach? If they've been through but can't talk about it, what good are they?

So if I could take a course on "Coaching" by John Wooden, a course on "Show Business" by Frank Sinatra, or a course on "The Pornography Business" by Ron Jeremy, they would not be allowed to use "war stories."

Makes sense to me.

It's funny because some highly sensitive and arrogant leader types don't want to hear "war stories" when it comes to information or training. Yet in war stories is where you find history, experience, and wisdom.

And then again, some so-called leaders don't have war stories, so that's a real problem if you look deeper into it.

The secret to leadership is caring. Caring about your people, caring about your agency, caring about your community, and caring about humanity.

It's kind of the same thing you'd find in an 8th-grade class anywhere in this country. It won't take very long for a student to figure out if the teacher cares … and if the teacher is a "leader."

Does the teacher care about the students, care about the student's learning environment, care about the student's work habits, and how each of them progresses?

That's a lot of things for a good teacher to care about, but that is what makes that teacher a "good leader" because they care.

"The stronger the law enforcement leadership ..., the safer the community."

If you have "strong" leadership in the place where you live, you will know it. The law enforcement leaders in your community will fulfill their commitment to your safety as strongly as you feel the need for your safety.

Leaders know what it takes to provide the community with an environment of safety. It just boils down to what your particular leadership is inclined to do and what their overall agenda is.

If the goal is to be politically correct and they allow the political atmosphere to determine how tough and effective they are on crime, they will be soft, and crime will go up. I use the terms tough and effective in the same sentence because crime and violence are very serious subjects. The tougher the stance you take on crime, the more effective overall you are. You become more effective because the people in the community notice that you are sincere and are not accepting excuses for bad behavior.

The people also need to know that the police will be there every day to protect them and make their neighborhoods safer. That's what they want, and that's what I would want.

I remember working the neighborhoods in Newton Division and the look on people's faces once they knew I would do whatever I could not to abandon them. I would do whatever I could to take away the fear that the local criminals would cast on the people as a way of exerting their power.

It becomes an issue of "trust" because although gang members in a given neighborhood might make up 5% of the population, they know they can rely on each other. The other 95% of the people who live there don't really know how much they can trust their neighbors and how far they would go for each other. Many times, people just want to mind their own business, and they stay safe that way.

That's what the gang members and criminals want … the neighbors not relying on each other. How else can 95% of the people be controlled by the less than 5%?

So when the law enforcement leadership is strong in a given neighborhood, the good people in that neighborhood become "stronger." But the catalyst has to be the law enforcement culture in that area. The people will follow the lead, but for that to happen, there must be trust. If trust does not exist, it's "every man for himself." I have to solve my own problems by keeping my family and myself out of harm's way.

An old timer once told me, "If you get through the academy and no one knows your name, that's what you want." Living in a crime-ridden neighborhood is much the same thing. If you can live day-to-day without any of the criminals and gang members noticing you or your family, that's good, right?

That's not a way to live.

In a large agency like the Los Angeles Police Department, the leadership, especially the captains and above, get moved around so much most of them do not make an impact in their position. They either don't have the time or are too busy trying not to make any mistakes so they can keep moving up the promotional ladder. That's great for their career but not so great for the leadership structure in some high-crime areas. It's also not great for the people living in those areas.

The people in these neighborhoods need a leader who will fiercely protect them and inspire those working under them to place a priority on true public safety. If that sort of passion does not exist in the leadership, don't expect a major change for the better in those officers working in that area.

That will not foster trust and confidence in the community, and for true "community engagement" to exist, the public must have faith in local law enforcement.

There's a reason why members of the community know certain officers who are expected to be there working day after day.

"People with pride do better work."

My last decade on the job, I supervised the department's "Gang Field Unit." Bob Ruchhoft, my Lieutenant when I was driving around in the yellow "Pac Man" car in the 1980s, brought me back there. He was now the Captain of the Division.

He told me he wanted to create a squad of officers that would work for gangs the way we did back in the 80s. This was now 1994, and violent crime had been rampant across the city at record levels for the past few years. He said, "I want you guys to make a difference."

I was able to pick two officers, and that was the beginning of the citywide "Gang Field Unit."

Over the next couple of years, we added officers and could successfully carry out vehicular surveillance operations. At that point, we were really good at following people and locating and arresting wanted criminals. Our mission was to seek out and apprehend the most dangerous and violent gang members and career criminals in the City of Los Angeles. The officers we were bringing in were excellent gang officers from around the department. We had talent. All our talent needed was support.

Here are a few points I focused on to make sure the members of our squad knew they were important and being supported –

- **Mission -** Our direction, goals, and mission were clear.
  We were to support divisional detectives by locating and apprehending suspects wanted for violent crimes committed

in the City of Los Angeles. We specialized in gang members because that's where much of our expertise was.

- **Importance-** I made our people understand that their work was important. Many of these suspects were hardcore criminals who would do anything to avoid being captured because they were looking at long prison sentences if caught. These cases were extremely difficult and dangerous. Safely bringing in any of these suspects was a "big deal."

- **Success -** I tried to make our unit successful by encouraging our members to "connect" with various detectives around the department. So, whenever a detective solved a case and was ready for an arrest, they would contact members of our unit to give them the first crack at the suspect before other officers and units started "beating the bushes" and potentially driving the suspect away. Divisional detectives normally didn't have the time and/or resources to track these suspects down themselves. We were successful because of the relationships we developed with the various detectives around the department and with other agencies.

- **Learning -** As the officer in charge of the Gang Field Unit, I encouraged their learning and development through training, meetings, conferences, and seminars. I believe the older you get and the more you learn, the better you get. The officers in our unit were also very good at teaching each other and training other law enforcement officers.

- **Recognition –** I tried to make sure that the unit received proper credit and recognition for their great work, and when anything came to light to our superiors involving our unit, it was something good.

  Any little bitches, headaches, and problems that popped up, we took care of ourselves. We kept rolling on and doing solid work. That became our reputation.

- **Care -** The members of our squad knew they were cared for. When a couple of our officers began driving their undercover cars like "Starsky and Hutch" on our surveillance, I put my foot down. I discouraged the crazy police car driving that was normal on a cop T.V. show. When one of our officers complained that we could lose the person we were following, my reply was, "So be it." Better to lose someone we're following than to have one of our officers run a red light and take out an innocent family in a car or kill themselves. We can always come back another day. Our people were more important than our mission ... and so were our families.

I believe that these factors provided an environment where the people in our unit had great pride in their work and their effectiveness.

That certainly affected how they went about doing their job on a day-to-day basis.

At one of our squad meetings, one of our officers said something that made me feel pretty good inside.

I created a three-page sheet listing a summary of the major arrests we had made during the prior 24-month period. It was pretty impressive and later got submitted for the LAPD's Meritorious Unit Award, which our unit did receive.

During our squad meeting, when I passed out a copy of the document to each member of our unit, one of the guys blurted out, "Damn ... I didn't know that we did this much. I just thought we were out there having a good time!"

We were ... and thank you for the compliment.

"I expect these three things from a frontline leader ...."

In 1996, I was supervising an LAPD citywide gang unit, and we were doing some work in Rampart Division. I was in Rampart Station using the restroom when I was approached by a Rampart Division supervisor. It was a guy I knew from a few years ago when he was a young officer working Newton Street Division. He was now a newly appointed sergeant assigned to Rampart.

Also, at this time, my oldest son had graduated from the L.A. Police Academy a few months earlier and was now also assigned to Rampart.

The sergeant said to me, "Tony, I have your son Ryan assigned to my squad. As his supervisor, what do you expect from me?

What can I do for him … and you?"

What a great question.

I thought about it for a couple of moments and replied to him, focusing on "three things."

Here are those" three things" in a longer version of what I said to him.

1. *Keep Him As Safe As Possible –*

The law enforcement career is inherently dangerous.

But there are ways to make the job even more dangerous than it is . Your mindset, your tactics, and your knowledge are a few of the things that can make the job safer. Not paying attention to those factors can make things more dangerous.

Especially with young officers, a supervisor, as well as a training officer, can set the stage for a young officer's attitude toward his or her job. Certain people can condition you for your entire career.

When I first got out of the academy in 1976, I had training officers and supervisors, but one officer stood out to me as being my mentor. He set the tone for my attitude as far as officer safety and my personal well-being were concerned. He taught me that when you get to a situation, any situation, the quicker you get "control," the safer you are. The quicker you get "control," the safer everyone is.

As I moved on in my career, I kept that theme in the back of my head, and it has diffused and gotten me out of more "hairy" situations than I can ever recount.

The other thing that I learned is that there are degrees of control. A suspect handcuffed is under control to a certain degree. But since bad things have happened to prisoners while they are handcuffed, it is only a degree of control. But the more" control" you have, the better.

The second component to being safe is your knowledge. The more you know, the safer you are. That being the case, you should never stop learning.

As I do law enforcement training, I still incorporate those two principles in my" Officer Safety" training.

In law enforcement, you can do everything right, and things can go wrong. What you are really doing in your training, tactics, and attitude is increasing the odds in your favor. That's the best we can do, and that's what I wanted for my son.

Keep him as safe as possible.

2. *Keep him out of trouble*

In law enforcement, there are many ways to get in trouble. You can do everything right and with a "good heart" and "good intentions" and get in trouble.

Supervision is not a popularity contest, nor is it meant to be. You need to have the courage to put your foot down with your people, even when they don't see or understand your decision.

Sometimes supervision is seeing what others cannot because of your experience. It's like looking at a pool of water and telling your people not to go in because you know what lurks below the surface … they don't.

Especially with younger officers, you, as a supervisor or training officer, have the power of influence over them, and you should not abuse that power. You can abuse that power by feeding your own ego and giving the false impression that you can get them out of any predicament. Sometimes officers aggressively marching forward to do their job can get in trouble, especially if they are led to believe there are no consequences for their behavior.

Knowing the rules, parameters, and boundaries is extremely important.

My last 13 years on the job, I supervised a plainclothes gang unit where our mission was to seek out and arrest gang members, and suspects wanted for committing violent crimes in the city of L.A.

We followed a lot of people (friends, relatives, sometimes the suspect themselves), and sometimes we would lose them or their vehicle. We had a new officer come into the unit, and on one operation, he was losing a vehicle we had been following in traffic, and he ran a red light, nearly causing a major traffic accident at a major intersection. As soon as I could, I pulled him aside and corrected his driving habits. He tried to resist my guidance and said, "But what if we lose him?"

I told him," This isn't T.V. The bigger picture is that the City of Los Angeles does not care. They are not going to back you're driving when you run a red light and kill a family on their way to church. Also, I'm not going to your house to tell your wife and kids that you died in a traffic accident trying to follow a possible relative of a possible suspect."

At the time, it takes courage to guide or correct one of your subordinates, but once they think about it, they understand that you care about them and that those are the rules. Play by the rules, but you can still play hard and be successful.

3. *Allow him to be successful and get better –*

Allowing him to be successful means many things. It's caring enough about him to keep him properly trained. It's holding him responsible for his basic daily duties.

It's developing within him an attitude of empathy, fairness, and strength.

Allow him to get his feet planted solidly under himself, learn the job step-by-step and apply what he has learned to constantly improve.

Allow him to become "solid" at what he does.

A law enforcement career is a very competitive career. Today's trainee can be in tomorrow's competition. The officer needs to gain self-confidence so that he or she can face the challenges with a proper frame of mind. Because life is governed by uncertainty, self-confidence enables the officer to face what comes with courage. That's part of the mental endurance that is sure to come in handy during a law enforcement career. Allow him to be as good as he can be.

I thanked the sergeant for "caring "enough to make my son the best he could be and for having the "courage" to correct him and guide him if he got out of line.

The mere act of this sergeant approaching me about my son let me know that he cared about his officers and that my son was in good hands.

These honest words of gratitude come from a fellow supervisor and cop … and, more importantly, a father.

"Leadership is content … not image."

Years ago, while I was supervising the Citywide Gang Field Unit, we got a visit from a gang supervisor who worked for a major metropolitan police department located in the eastern United States. I won't mention his department, and you'll soon understand why.

He jumped in with me, and we drove down to Southeast Station in Watts because that's where our unit's operation was going to happen.

We were going to be looking for a gang member that had committed several-armed robberies.

The supervisor was a real nice guy and enjoyed touring around Los Angeles, especially some of the gang areas. We got to Southeast Station about 3:30 pm in time to see the change of watch in the parking lot where the officers working Day Watch were coming to the station to be relieved by the officers that were working Night Watch.

So, there were a lot of uniform patrol officers going to and from the station.

The supervisor was very impressed with the appearance of the officers. Everybody, for the most part, looked neat and clean, with no goatees, long hair, or ponytails on the male officers, like the supervisor's department of origin. For the most part, the officers looked very sharp and in shape on this average LAPD patrol day.

We completed our unit briefing in the parking lot, away from the rest of the officers and foot traffic. We discussed assignments, the suspect, the location, and what we expected to happen if we were to be successful on this day.

When the supervisor and I got back into my car, his jaw dropped. I came to find out where he worked, and a supervisor would not be involved in the takedown and arrest. He and the other supervisors would stay away until either the suspect was arrested or the operation came to an end for whatever reason.

He looked at me like I was either crazy or stupid and wanted to know the reasoning of having a supervisor present during a field operation.

I explained to him that as their supervisor, one of my responsibilities (among a few others) was to ensure that the team could be successful in their endeavors. Since I had a lot of experience and was the person in charge, I thought of myself as more of a player/coach. The mission we were charged with was difficult, and each operation had its own unique set of circumstances.

As a "player/coach," I was more of an overseer, and with most of these dangerous suspects, the more experienced minds, the better. By no means were these operations a one-man show, and every team member had input; decisions were made at very crucial times. I couldn't see myself sitting in the office while something bad might occur.

Plus, as an on-scene supervisor, I could clear the way for our people to do their work and not deal with obstacles as they popped up, such as other officers, other agencies, and command staff, especially when something did go down, such as an arrest. Most of our suspects were located in divisions other than jurisdictions in which they originally committed the crime they were wanted for.

In some incidents, a supervisor was necessary to smooth over any number of issues. That should be the job of the person in charge, and that is part of a leader taking care of his or her people.

These were things that probably had never crossed the supervisor's mind before. Or maybe things he had never concerned himself with. Luckily for me, I was taught by the best and had the opportunity to see the best in action as it pertains to frontline leadership.

I would much rather take part in the grind and be involved in the actual process than have my picture taken at the podium after the fact at a press conference. With leadership, there is "frosting," and there is "cake." The frosting is sort of the image of the cake; some cakes look way better than they taste.

In leadership, the important part is the cake … not the frosting.

"One-dimensional leadership" is really at the core of the morale problems plaguing today's law enforcement officers.

"One-dimensional leadership" is management's practice of using intellectuals and academics to design their strategies for solving policing issues. These are well-educated people who have little or no actual hands-on, practical experience in police work. They don't do the actual job. They are well-respected students of policing whose philosophies and theories are blessed by management.

Some ideas are good, and some are not so good. This creates serious morale problems because those officers who actually do the job are not consulted for their input prior to the implementation of a strategy.

The "elite" of law enforcement leaders have a collection of lobbyists, consulting firms, and think tanks that provide research and strategies for policing. The knowledge or input of the experienced frontline officers who actually do the job is rarely considered. The coach isn't putting his "best player" in the game.

It's ironic because many of today's "innovators" use the theme of returning to the "cop on the beat" method of community policing.

That is because the "cop on the beat" understood the job, the people, and their problems. Yet in today's intellectual environment, that actual "cop on the beat" would not be consulted for his unique wisdom and knowledge.

Police work can be a dirty, nasty, and unpleasant job.

Few people possess the mental endurance needed to be successful at it. Today's frontline officers are considered at the bottom of law enforcement's food chain due to their assignment and the rank connected with that assignment.

Officers do not feel appreciated by their bosses for the difficult job they do.

For a police executive to tell a group of officers to "dump the warrior mentality" and adopt a "guardian" mindset is demeaning and lacks insight. During a normal shift, a patrol officer will wear many hats depending on the situation.

That officer may be a counselor, teacher, parent, adviser, referee, babysitter, mediator, or coach. "Warrior" and "guardian" are just two more of the many roles the frontline officer must fulfill.

In talking to frontline officers, I can tell you that many are upset, resentful, and frustrated by management's lack of concern and respect for them. Everyone else's opinion about their job seems to be more important.

The spirit of doing police work is being sucked right out of officers by the leadership they perceive doesn't respect or support them and caters to public opinion, which is the "easy way out." This is a serious problem.

One solution is a balanced mix of intellectual ideas, and theories blended with the valued wisdom and experience that can only come from the frontline. Put those highly educated minds in a room with seasoned, battle-scarred veteran cops and watch the real innovation begin. Add another dimension to the problem-solving process by including insight, ideas, and knowledge that come from experienced officers.

You stand a better chance of winning by putting your "best player" in the game.

"You won't have the courage to find the solution if you don't have the courage to face the problem."

I was once watching the Dr. Phil Show, and it was a segment where the guest was a woman who had been molested by her grandfather over the course of a few years when she was a child.

Her horrible story was painful enough to hear, but then they spoke with another guest on the show. It was the woman's grandmother. The grandmother allegedly didn't realize that the molestation was occurring, even though, as stated, it went on for a few years. The grandmother seemed sincerely sorrowful that she hadn't detected a problem with her husband's behavior toward his granddaughter. However, the woman who was the actual victim of years and years of molestation wasn't buying her grandmother's theatrics.

The reason for the victim's hostility towards her grandmother was that on one occasion, the grandmother walked into the bedroom as the grandfather was in the act of molesting his granddaughter. The grandmother observed what was occurring and abruptly walked out of the room, almost in embarrassment.

When questioned about that allegation by Dr. Phil, the grandmother stated that she wasn't actually sure what was going on and walked out, even though both grandfather and grandchild had portions of their clothing removed.

At that point in time, that grandmother chose not to acknowledge that there was a problem. That woman was in extreme denial, and because of that, she allowed her granddaughter to suffer years of sexual molestation at the hands of the child's grandfather, the woman's husband.

If we believe the grandmother's logic for her response and behavior, she didn't realize there was a problem, and because no problem was detected, there was no solution.

No problem … no solution.

Problems come in all shapes and sizes. Some "leaders" seem to specialize in handling the little, lightweight issues and sidestepping the big ones … or at least look the other way as the grandmother did that day with her husband and granddaughter.

True leaders are there no matter the problem or issue and don't duck the tough fights. That's why true leadership is a pleasure to watch. That's why in the law enforcement world, the majority of the "true leaders" are actually out on the frontline, "truly leading." They are not primarily focused on promoting.

We were once involved in trying to arrest a gang member that was wanted for numerous murders. During the course of the confrontation with this suspect, my yellow "Pac-Man" police car rammed the suspect's vehicle, and the armed suspect was shot numerous times and killed.

As this was occurring, there was a veteran patrol training officer with his rookie partner just out of the academy who was handling a radio call just a block away. The training officer had 12 years on the job and was a squared-away individual that I knew from working in the area.

Seconds after the shooting, the officer and his partner rolled up, and he approached me and asked me what had occurred. I explained to him the situation, and he asked what I needed. I told him, and he said he would handle it.

At that moment, that officer took control of the situation, helping to secure the scene and the crowd and directing the incoming personnel where to go and what to do. To me, it was as though the clouds in the dark night sky opened up, and a light shined down on this training officer. He became the ringmaster.

This training officer was not technically a supervisor by LAPD standards, but he stepped up and took charge of what we needed him to do.

He had the experience, knowledge, and courage to step forward and apply his talent to successfully help take control of a chaotic situation.

Even as supervisors, detectives, and command staff officers arrived at the scene, this officer was on his job, providing people with the information they needed to know and directing people to where they needed to go. Obviously, as things settled down, the "structured" chain of command settled in and took over.

But in those immediate crucial moments when the tough decisions are made, that officer stepped up and displayed true leadership and his value to his department.

You won't see that kind of leadership hanging on a certificate from some leadership school on some wall in some office in some building somewhere.

It's the kind of leadership that only the people around him can see and the type of leader that will step up and tackle a problem.

Don't be the type of person that makes rank by avoiding leadership.

"You can write a book on being a lion tamer ... but have you ever been in a cage with a real lion?"

A friend of mine once told me after going to a very famous law enforcement leadership academy, "You know ... they don't want their facilitators telling war stories." He knew he would get a rise out of me.

"No war stories?

Probably because they don't have any," was my reply.

So, what they are saying is that if they could have John Wooden teach a class on coaching, Frank Sinatra teach a class on show business, or Ron Jeremy teach a class on the porn industry, you wouldn't want any of them to tell" war stories. "What would be the point in having them teach if they couldn't tell the students what life was like where they were viewing it from?

That's where the "big equalizer" comes in. Many academies, schools, and educational law enforcement programs will settle instructors who may have experience teaching but no experience in the subject matter being taught. To me, especially in the law enforcement world, you want instructors who have "been there...

done that"; otherwise, how do you know what works and what doesn't.

First of all, being an instructor and a "law enforcement instructor' at that is tough. You expose yourself, putting yourself out there in what is a very competitive field. Part of the competitive nature of law enforcement officers is to compare themselves to their peers. You might want to be like them, be better than them or just fit in with the crowd. You can feel like you're always being judged, so why would anyone volunteer for "extra" judgment. I guess that's part of the competition.

Credibility is a major concern with any law enforcement instructor because it normally comes down to "Where have you been?" and "What have you done?" Why would any "leadership academy" not want their instructors to have "war stories"? Because those war stories validate credibility so, to me, they are selling their attendees a "bill of goods." They are more concerned with their prestige, image, and reputation than their product.

Some of the best instructors and classes I have heard over the years made a mental impact on me due to their war stories because they are easier to remember and usually have a valuable lesson attached to them.

I understand not wanting the attendees to sit there and listen to your "old drunk uncle" talk about how things were "back in the day." But I do think most of today's instructors are more effective and savvy than to let the train run off the tracks in that direction.

For any instructor, communication is key, so if you can get your point across and do it in an effective manner, why not? But to discourage war stories from your instructors sounds more like an insecurity issue than a competent way to teach a class.

"Meet Mr. Freeze ... or 'things are fine just as they are. "
One of the people I met while writing this book relayed the following story to me. This was a person that I worked for a few times during my career and someone that I highly respect.

He was a lieutenant in a division that focused on gathering and disseminating intelligence information on criminal organizations. Though it wasn't necessarily a high-stress type of assignment, the nature of the information was sensitive and confidential. Everything was on a "need to know "basis. A captain headed the division, and he had four lieutenants working directly under him. In total, there were about fifty investigators assigned to the unit.

The Captain of this division had been assigned there for quite a few years and basically did things his way. He was very particular about who was brought into the unit and how they conducted their work. He was not very trusting and had a couple of favorites which he closely confided in.

Everyone else was a second-class citizen in the unit. He was very serious about all matters pertaining to the job and did not have a sense of humor. He was not very inspiring because he really didn't trust too many people, so communication with him was minimal. He pretty much kept himself locked up inside his office, hardly ever interacting or socializing with the troops.

So my lieutenant friend found himself as the acting Commanding Officer in Charge (OIC) of the division for one week as our regular Captain was away on a short vacation.

One of the luxuries of being the man in charge for one week is that you get to occupy the Captain's office during that time. So now the Lieutenant would get to see all of the stuff that kept the Captain busy on a day-to-day basis. He would get to see why the guy was too busy to interact with his people and all of the "hot stuff" he couldn't share with others.

To further set up this scenario, I must tell you that the Captain in question was some type of English language expert in college and was a real stickler for grammar and spelling on all reports. I can understand that because you don't want official police reports showing up in court or some other venue with misspelled words and written words that didn't make sense. You want things to appear professional. This Captain's signature trademark for correcting reports or adding emphasis to certain parts of the department's orders and directives was to mark the document with a green felt marker. You didn't want something in your private box with green markings on it because it usually meant that you screwed up or needed to pay closer attention to something.

As the lieutenant took over the captain's office on the first day, he sat back in the captain's chair and noticed huge stacks of magazines on a bookshelf. This was not unusual because when you are responsible for keeping current on information involving criminal organizations, one of the things you do is to keep track of articles that appear in newspapers and magazines. Information is wherever you can get it.

So, the acting OIC lieutenant got through the various things that cross that captain's desk on a daily basis in about an hour. In his boredom, the lieutenant started browsing through some of the magazines so he could stay up on current affairs. He opened a couple of the magazines, and to his disbelief, he discovered that the articles he was looking at had been "green-lined."

The lieutenant then began looking through other magazines and periodicals in the office and discovered that everything had been green-lined. This captain, the head of a critical entity within a large metropolitan police department, spent the majority of his days reading magazines and looking to correct them for spelling and grammatical errors.

So you are heading a specialized unit with about 60 employees, and the best you can do is to lock yourself in your office most of the day and keep to yourself. This sends a loud and clear message to everyone that you don't give a crap about your people and what they are doing.

This pretty much fits his description of him before I got there and started to contemplate transferring to that unit.

When I was working in this unit, the attitude on the part of most of us was that he was the mean, old-fashioned, and not real bright father, and we were the slick kids always trying to get one by old "pops." The leadership of our "boss" was basically non-existent, and we would make him think he was running things by strictly adhering to all of his quirks and rules. But basically, he didn't have a clue on what was actually going on in his unit. It would be fine with him if nothing ever happened in the division and no one ever had anything to say. He would justify the "nothingness" by commenting about how sensitive and confidential the cases were that his people were working on.

"The only man who never makes a mistake is the man who never does anything." - Theodore Roosevelt.

"Motivation is motivation … wherever you can get it."

So, I showed up this particular morning at the Panera Restaurant in the city of Whittier, and I knew it would be a good day. The person I was looking for was sitting there all alone as if he were waiting for me.

About a year earlier, I left the gym and went into that Panera for some after-work out food and drink. While there, I see a familiar face from my old days at the LAPD. It was George "Pelon" Spitzer, a legendary Assistant Watch Commander at Hollenbeck Division. Although I never had the pleasure of working for Sergeant Spitzer, I casually made his acquaintance over the years. However, I personally knew countless officers that were either saved and/or straightened out by him.

Spitzer was the type of "dinosaur" sergeant that brought out the insecurities from some of the supervisors and superior officers around him. The reason he did that was because the troops respected and gravitated towards him. They had trust in him and knew that he always had their best interest in mind. You may not like what you would hear coming from him, but if it was what was best for you, you were going to hear it.

As I saw "Sarge" sitting by himself in the café, I thought to myself, "What a waste." What a waste that here you have a man who is a master at dealing with and handling people, a true leader of men, and he is sitting here all alone. Meanwhile, across the land, you have professionals being sent to various leadership training sessions and classes, many of which are taught by paper managers, not true leaders in the sense of the word. The man who should be teaching these classes and being recognized for his proven leadership skills sits alone, unnoticed, and ignored. What a waste of knowledge and wisdom.

I approached Sergeant Spitzer and introduced myself. He remembered me from his cop days. I explained to him that I was retired and working on a book about supervision and leadership. I also told him that I would be honored if I could sit down with him sometime for about an hour and pick his brain about leadership, supervision, and the qualities of a good leader. He agreed and figured I would catch him sometime when it was convenient for the both of us.

I would see him from time to time at Panera, and I even saw him at a funeral for a mutual cop friend of ours that had passed away. Spitzer stayed in the back of my mind, and as I got more serious about this book, meeting with him became more of a priority.

While at a funeral for a family member, I ran into another former LAPD acquaintance that I also met with in putting this book together. I mentioned George Spitzer to him, and he told me, "Tony, whatever you do, don't miss out on talking to George for your book. That's real wisdom."

So, as I drove down to Panera on this day and saw smiling George sitting there alone, I knew this was a good day.

We were discussing various subjects pertaining to the book, and I asked him, "Who was the worst boss you ever worked for?"

To my surprise, Spitzer identified the same lieutenant who I had disliked because, early in my career, he kept me from getting into a CRASH unit he supervised. The lieutenant didn't know me, but he didn't like me, so that was that. I later asked a friend of mine that worked for him why he wouldn't let me in the unit, and he thought I was "out of control" and hard to supervise. I meant nothing to him and wasn't worth the risk to the peace and quiet of his unit.

Spitzer told me that he almost punched the lieutenant out a couple of times because the guy was selfish, didn't care about his people, was more concerned about the "image" of his unit, and was real "one-way." In other words, do as I say and not as you see me do. Everything he did was for himself. Not very well-liked, but people did like working his unit. The five divisions comprising Central Bureau ... Central, Hollenbeck, Newton Street, Northeast, and Rampart had plenty of gangs and plenty of girls if you were so inclined. The officers that worked for him just stayed out of his way, which isn't hard to do working for a do-nothing jerk.

Spitzer also told me that the worse part of the lieutenant was that he was a hypocrite. He had rules for "his people" and rules for himself, and obviously, they weren't the same. And the worse part is that he was open about the discrepancy, so if you wanted to work his unit, you had to put up with the hypocrisy. He had a bad reputation, but he didn't care. He didn't care about anything but himself and certainly didn't care about the people around him. Like

I said, he almost got his nose broken a couple of times, but it never happened.

The good thing about not working for him was that he had no control over me. I knew the gangs in the Newton Street Division area pretty well, but if you want to see someone out of control, I'll show you someone "out of control." It doesn't take much to feed that reputation.

I knew some of the people working in his unit and had some good working relationships. In one case, the detectives were looking for a gun that was used in a shooting and heard that it might be in some gangster's residence. The detectives said they didn't have enough probable cause to "get in" the gangster's house with a warrant and look, so they were stuck. I told them that I could get in with no warrant.

I knew this gangster's mom pretty well, so my partner and I went to the residence. We door knocked, and she answered. I told her why we were there, and she gave us consent to search the entire residence. The kid who was not there was a "thug," but his mom, who I respected, had tried to do a good job of keeping her eye on him. Because of his nosey mom, I didn't think that any gun or contraband would be there, and they weren't.

Back then, in the 1980s, not everyone had a cell phone like we all do now. I called the detective's office and asked for them. Their supervisor answered the phone and said they weren't there. He asked me if I wanted to leave a message, and I said, "Yes. This is Officer Moreno, and I'm in the Smith residence. Tell them that is no gun here."

The supervisor flipped out. He was aware of their case and the problem they had trying to get a search warrant for the residence. He said, "You're in there now!"

I said, "Yep … and no gun here."

I was helping these detectives out, but I inadvertently added to my reputation of being "out of control" with this little stunt. The supervisor was highly upset and pissed off.   I'm sure he then ran to the lieutenant with the scenario, and my reputation grew. While everyone was flipping out, the detectives returned to their station. When their supervisor told them what I had done, they said, "Yeah … we asked him to. He did us a favor."

I thought it was in the spirit of one of our (LAPD's) 20 Departmental Management Principles #14, "Police Working with Police." The supervisor, who didn't know me very well and didn't trust me, did not like the way this whole thing went down. But it wasn't up to him. It was up to the detectives handling the case. They asked me for a favor regarding a gang member that I knew real well, and I did what I did for them. I think his issue was that they didn't run it by him first. Meanwhile, his boss, the lieutenant, just saw me as more and more "out of control."

I remember that one more incident happened with that lieutenant. A couple of months later, some other detectives in that same unit were looking for a gang member wanted for murder. They were looking high and low for him, and he had apparently gotten away from some officers in that unit a couple of times. The detectives were frustrated, and one of them contacted me and told me that the gang member in question was wanted for murder and was considered "armed and dangerous." I told him that his lieutenant wouldn't be too happy if I bought his suspect in, and he said, "Fuck him! We need to get a murderer off the street."

By now, I had transferred out of Newton Street Division and got a job at DSD/ Gangs, which was a citywide gang unit, and it turned out to be a much better job for me. The CRASH units back then were assigned to a Bureau, and each Bureau had 4-5 divisions under it. My new unit was a citywide unit, and I could go anywhere and help anyone. I was also assigned this yellow Plymouth Fury that no one else wanted. The guys in the unit called it "the banana." I didn't care about that. Just give me the car . I drove it for the next five years with a couple of different partners, and that is how the original "Pac-Man" was born.

I knew this gang member really well, and one day my partner and I saw him driving a car in Newton Division. It was in the afternoon, and there just happened to be an LAPD air unit up in the sky over Newton Division, where we were. We contacted him and told him we had a 187 (murder) suspect in a vehicle, and they responded in seconds.

The suspect drove southbound to Hooper Avenue, passing 55th Street and picking up speed. He made a left turn on 56th Street, and we were on him. I knew him real well and knew he would run if he had the chance. Then he made a tactical mistake …he pulled to the left into the driveway of a residence. He was about to exit the car when I pulled up to his door with the Pac-Man car. The air unit, by now, had other patrol units responding to our location to assist us.

As he opened the car door, the suspect," Fred," as we'll call him, looked at me, and he knew he was fucked. He put his hands up and complied with our orders, and was taken into custody without any further incident. I don't advise anybody to pull up to the driver's door in the police vehicle next to a vehicle containing a murder suspect, but this was one of those unique situations where it worked. When he pulled into the driveway, he couldn't go any further forward, and he wasn't going to back out of there. The only chance he had was to bail out of the car and outrun us, which he would have done. I used our vehicle to cut off his escape route. He didn't expect that and was overwhelmed by our unexpected actions.

I knew when we showed up at the CRASH office with Fred in tow, it was really going mind-fuck the lieutenant. But I had to make one stop on the way to the CRASH office. Fred's fellow gang members would congregate at 55th Street and Ascot Avenue, and the past couple of days, we'd drive by the group and ask them, "Anybody seen Fred?" This went on for about a week.

Now that we had Fred in custody, I thought I'd play a trick on his homeboys. Leaving the scene of the arrest, I had Fred lay down in the back seat of our yellow Pac-Man vehicle. We drove by where his homeboys were hanging out, and I pulled up and said, "Anybody seen Fred?"

They laughed, and some of them looked all around the bushes, under cars, and one even looked in his pants pockets, but no Fred. One said, "Sorry, Pac-Man, we haven't seen him around."

At that moment, I told Fred to sit up in the back seat, and I said to the group, "Here he goes right here!" pointing to Fred in the backseat of our car.

You haven't lived until you've seen the jaws of 7 or 8 hardcore gang members all drop at one time in unison. They were all speechless. Then I said, "We'll see you all later," and we drove off towards downtown with Fred safely in tow.

We weren't done with Fred, though. We still had to take him to the CRASH detectives who had his case. This meant going to that lieutenant's office and delivering the goods. I must admit it filled me with some satisfaction. The only problem was with a couple of officers that Fred got away from originally … in fact, he got away from them a couple of times.

Once we got to the office, there were a lot of people there because this was late afternoon on a weekday. We went to the front desk and asked for the detectives who were there. We were waiting for them when the lieutenant walked in, looked at our suspect, looked at us, and went into his office semi slamming the door behind him. He got the message, "We are here to help."

We downplayed the arrest of Fred because I didn't want to make too many enemies of the officers working CRASH. I had friends working there, but I also had a couple of "haters" and didn't want to encourage their hatred. You know, "We got lucky, and the air unit just happened to be there with us, so he just gave up."

What's interesting about this portion of the book is that I started out interviewing "a true leader" about the worse "leader" he had ever encountered in his career. This had nothing to do with me. But when you take into consideration that Sergeant Spitzer had a military career and then a long and prestigious LAPD career and if you think about all of the hundreds of "leaders" he has encountered in his life, what are the odds that he would have picked the same guy I had picked.

Sergeant Spitzer and I never worked together. Our careers would cross paths every now and then when we were working in Hollenbeck Division, but I knew he was a "true and solid leader." When he was on duty as the Assistant Watch Commander, he was the "king of the station" and really knew his stuff. What was really good about him was that he would go above and beyond to help certain employees, sometimes when they were too stupid to help themselves. He saved a lot of people some grief because he cared.

Spitzer and I didn't look at life through the same set of eyes, but that's why the both of us picking the same lieutenant as the worst supervisor we had ever encountered was truly amazing. The lieutenant was so bad that the people who worked for him had to learn how to handle him so that his ineptness couldn't hurt them. Luckily, he was dumb enough so that he could be "handled."

That's two of us with many years of experience picking out the same guy as "the worst." He should probably get an award or something. But the good thing is that he and other "leaders" like him have inspired a great many people like me "not to be like him." Sometimes that example is better than any leadership lesson or course.

Self-improvement is about constant motivation.

Motivation is motivation wherever you can get it.

"You Can Send A Duck To Eagle School ... But You Just Get A Fancy Duck."

(This title of this topic is in reference to the book "You Can't Send A Duck To Eagle School" written by Mac Anderson)

Leadership isn't something that can be taught, bought, inherited, or sold. It is the courage to do the right thing even when it isn't the best thing for you. For this reason, a lot of high-ranking officers are not really leaders. They are selfish enough to promote but not courageous enough to do the right thing at the expense of their own careers.

Sometimes in law enforcement, you'll get to a fork in the road where you have to ask yourself, "Do I want a job with a higher rank, higher pay, and more prestige, or do I want a job where I can do what I love doing, working and doing what I do best leading on the frontline?"

I know that coming from a very large police department, the higher you go in rank, the further away you get from the action on the frontline. You can actually get pretty far away, so far that many high-ranking and command staff officers forget where they once worked ... on the frontline.

I personally put more stock into doing the work I enjoyed doing. I liked being able to see the actual difference being made. I liked the camaraderie of working around fellow officers and working as a team to accomplish a goal. In the latter part of my career, I supervised a surveillance unit that would go out and, as I put it, "surgically remove violent criminals from the community." I retired as a detective supervisor, and I was happy with that.

If I had chosen to move up in the rank structure of the department, it would have pulled me away from the actual frontline work. Although having increased responsibility over more officers and personnel, it would also have meant being more of an administrator than a "cop."

The best "leaders" I have worked for who held those high-ranking positions had one thing in common … they cared about their people. And in caring about their people, they never forgot their roots and where they came from, and just how difficult working on the frontline is.

I think that those compassionate qualities in a sound leader are inherent in certain people and can't be learned. With most good leaders, they handle their personal lives as they do their professional ones. Maybe some of those qualities can be "improved upon," but I don't believe that you can change a person's nature by sending them to management training or leadership school. That type of training might make a true leader better, but it won't necessarily create a leader.

That's why I'm not overly impressed with rank, plaques, certificates, and other awards in regard to leadership. In fact, send a lousy leader to a one-week leadership school, give him a certificate, and he'll probably be more convinced that his substandard way of doing things is the right way, or he wouldn't be rewarded for his management skills. The system is kind of making "leadership monsters."

Evidence of what I am talking about is the current state of law enforcement and its relationship with the community. Our leaders cater to public opinion, or "perceived" public opinion, and neglect the quiet, the silent majority. This gives the perception of a weak law enforcement bent on pacifying certain individuals and groups while giving away the peace and order of the community. That's why violent crime is up all over the country. This has created a "culture of defiance" and has given criminals and gang members more room to operate.

Where did our leadership learn to take the easy way out at the expense of the law-abiding citizens in our communities? Why did our leaders, over 130 police chiefs and managers, recently meet in Chicago to seek methods to reduce the prison population? Why wasn't this meeting to find solutions to make it more difficult for criminals to victimize our citizens?

Maybe the issue isn't sending ducks to eagle school. Maybe the real issue is to ensure that the "true eagles" are put in the position to attend "eagle school."

"Here's my leadership advice"

- **Make things better** – Don't be critical, nitpick, or dog people. Try to make things better and show how they can be done. I've always felt that super-critical supervisors were insecure about themselves and just trying to level the playing field.

- **Respect your team** – Everybody who works for you is a real person. Treat them as such and have regard for their thoughts, words, and actions. You respect them, and they will respect you.

- **Enjoy your job** – The more you enjoy your job, the more people will like being around you and working for you. The negative, sour, and pessimistic boss sucks the life out of the room, and that attitude is contagious.

- **Be a positive force for all** – Be a positive force by listening to people, understanding them, and encouraging them. It sounds corny, but you have to be the light during darkness. People will follow the light.

- **Serve everyone** – Don't play favorites or be unfair with your treatment of people. You may not even be aware of that perception, and that is why you need to keep checking yourself.

- **Do not rest on your laurels** – It doesn't matter how good of a cop you were because they already know about you. Your job is to be a leader and not rub your success in other people's faces. You're either insecure or arrogant ... and neither one is good.

- **Don't ask someone to do something you wouldn't do yourself** – Part of the credibility of a leader is that he won't ask others to do what he wouldn't do himself. His credibility is that he probably has already done it himself.

- **Be approachable** – As the vice-principal said to me in another part of the book, always listen to people because you never know what they're going to say. Be open and caring, and conduct yourself with discretion. They will come to you.

- **Rise above the challenge** – Focus on what you're trying to accomplish. If you fail or have trouble succeeding, find another way to accomplish your objective. If there is a way, the true leader will find it. Use your people to find the solution.

- **Think of the long-term effect** – It's your vision. You have to look ahead, plot out your strategy and think, taking the future into consideration. Think in terms of stability, consistency, and endurance.

- **Set the example** – You be the model for those working around you. You set the bar and the expectations for them by exactly being what you want from them. If they can see it in you, they can do it.

- **Don't give up your principles in the face of controversy** — Stay true to who you are by not caving into professional and political pressure. Sometimes this is the hill that the leader "dies on." This is why you are paid more money and given more responsibility. This decision is yours.

It's as simple as the quote by Simon Sinek at the beginning of this chapter ... Leaders eat last ...."

Chapter 5 - Officer Safety and Tactics

"You're not paid to be the biggest, baddest, or strongest out there. You're paid to be the smartest."– Tony "Pac-Man" Moreno

"You Don't Know What You Don't Know ... Until You Find Out."

I've met a lot of great cops over the years and others that think they are better than they really are. If there's one field of work where you don't want to be overconfident, it's in law enforcement. You get overconfident when things get too easy, too normal, or when it takes little effort to be successful. Those are all signs of a "big head," and that affects your attitude.

A good friend of mine was coordinating a gang conference where he expected about 220 attendees. It was a 2-day conference, so there would be plenty of networking between classes and at the social functions connected to the event. But he told me that he fielded a couple of calls that disappointed him because the caller wanted to know who was going to be there attending the classes in order to get an idea of how much partying they would be doing. He said that those couple of callers had no interest in getting better; they wanted to "party."

I'm not a "party-pooper," but anyone who pays good money to go to a conference and mainly wants to party had better hope that he or she is as good as they think they are ... and that they don't have that much to learn.

I really do believe that finding young people who really want to be good officers or gang cops is getting harder and harder. I think that is because it's not as fashionable nowadays to be an avid learner of a particular skill. You aren't cool if you don't already know. Who needs to learn?

The truth is "learning" is a skill. There are many ways to learn, but one of the best is to simply ask because it is "direct," and you can be specific about what you want to know. Nothing is as refreshing as a young person asking for my opinion about an issue or situation they are faced with. That person wants to learn.

In my training, I mentioned a scenario when I was a young officer, and I asked an "old-timer" working gangs a question about a particular gang. His response was, "Why do you want to know?"

I tell the attendees in my training classes that when that happens, you have encountered an "asshole." That's a person that is threatened by you, and you want to learn about "his gang." He may give you a crumb here and there, but the fact that he doesn't want you to know as much as he knows in a dangerous world makes him an "asshole."

That is why, as I became knowledgeable working gangs, I really tried not to rely on other officers for my information. I had my network, and I knew who to trust, but as time went on, I just refused to depend on some of those "insecure experts" for their knowledge or input. I would rather have people asking me for information which I would gladly share. We are supposed to make each other better and safer.

Which leads me back to the title of this section. "You don't know what you don't know … until you find out."

In law enforcement, as in life, you should always strive to learn because there is always more to learn. You stop learning … you stop living. But in law enforcement, it can be critical and even deadly not to have certain knowledge. Shame is when there is a certain fact or fact you could have known but didn't that would have made a difference. That is when you finally figure out that there are things out there you really don't know, and by the time you realize that it's too late.

Don't be overconfident in your knowledge because "sometimes we finish the exam … and sometimes the exam finishes us."

"Who Is More Dedicated … You Or Your Opponent?"

When training law enforcement officers, I bring up this topic accompanied by a photo of a gang member I took at Tamara Prison in Tegucigalpa, Honduras. The gang member's face is covered with tattoos, most of them gang tattoos giving him a very sinister and intimidating look.

I follow up with the comment, "I notice that none of you have your agency or unit tattooed on your face. Does that mean that this gang member is more dedicated than you?"

That answer should be "no," but looking at that gang member with tattoos can make one wonder who is more dedicated, him or you? To me, dedication is a mental state that measures commitment to a task or cause, like a job or mission.

To analyze my level of dedication, you'd have to cut me open and take parts of my heart, brain, and soul to get an accurate reading. You can't measure my dedication by reading my forehead. To me, that's just a prop or tool to help gain a psychological advantage over another person. With gang members and the general public, it works.

I have learned over the years to focus on the task at hand of gaining control of a situation by using sound tactics and methods. When everyone is under control and things are safe, I may then check out any unique or noteworthy characteristics, such as tattoos.

But I don't let people have a psychological edge over me by using their props. That's a decision and mindset developed ahead of time, so when pulling a car over and a scary monster exits, you're not covering your eyes and cowering like a frightened child.

When the scary monster gets out of his car, and he sees that I'm not distracted by his "look" and I'm taking care of business, he will know that I am as dedicated to my cause as he is to his, probably more so. No punks here …

"Two Things Can Erase Fear … They Are 'Anger' And 'Focus'".

It's been my experience that the mind has two ways to overcome fear. This is very important for officer safety because encountering situations that can produce fear is part of the job. Those two qualities that act as erasers are "anger" and "focus."

Anger can overcome fear, but anger is an emotional response that can make a person "undisciplined." At that point, it can alter judgment and cause personal harm. There were numerous instances when an officer used anger to overcome a situation. The problem is that an officer's anger can get him in trouble. So even though you may have met a dangerous challenge with anger and prevailed, the anger can cause a bigger issue than the original problem, to begin with. That is why a solid partner or supervisor can help keep an angry officer out of trouble.

Focus can also overcome fear, but it is "disciplined" and can be a guide through dangerous and critical situations.

Focus is relying on experience, training, proficiency, and mental strength to be at your best. The goal or object of your actions is to use your talent to complete your mission,

Focus on the task at hand, whether it is a carload of gang members being pulled over, a combative inmate being extracted from a cell, or the front door on a narcotic search warrant being breached.

Focus brings all of those positive qualities together. The more prepared, the sharper the focus will be. The sharper the focus, the better you will handle the stress, pressure, and challenge of the situation. That's what a professional, seasoned officer does.

Focus is you rely on your own experience, training, self-discipline, and mental strength to be at your best.

Anger is an emotion that needs to be controlled and kept in check. Focus is the method by which you operate and do the job and should only improve with time.

Anger is not your friend and will cause you to lose control of your emotions and self-discipline. When that happens in the heart of the battle, you make mistakes. Those mistakes can cause you to lose your career, your freedom, or your life. Trust me, If you have a sufficient amount of focus, you won't need anger.

There will be moments when you'll look back on a certain situation and ask yourself, "Wow, how did I do that?"   It was the focus, my friend.

"The More You Know, The Safer You Are."

If you were going to use an ATM at night to withdraw some cash and you knew at this particular ATM, two guys were going to rob you and shoot you; you'd probably use a different ATM.

If you knew that on a Sunday morning, while driving to church and passing through a certain intersection, an elderly lady in her vehicle was going to run a red light and smash your car, you'd probably take a different route.

Those are two examples of information if you had would make you much safer. It may not really matter how that information finds you because there are countless ways to gain and receive information. But now that you have the information, you can use it.

Information is the raw data received and refined to solve a case, answer a question on a test, or determine if a person is right for you. Information is processed through your brain to determine how useful it is. The more information used and developed, the more experience and success acquired. This should be an ongoing process and will continue throughout your personal and professional life.

Based on this philosophy, too much information is better than not enough. I can have tons of information, but if I can sort through and figure out that the elderly lady is going to run that red light, that tiny bit of information may have saved my life.

On the other hand, if I never receive the information about the elderly lady in her car, it won't help me, and I am at the mercy of my fate. Law enforcement can do everything right, and things can still go wrong. With training, experience, and knowledge, the best we can do is put the odds a little more in our favor.

How you deal with coworkers, superiors, subordinates, suspects, or the public, attitude, and personality will have a significant effect on whether you are receiving information or not. If people don't like you or are uncomfortable being around you, overall effectiveness is weakened.

I have been around officers who sincerely didn't care what their coworkers or members of the public thought of them. That's fine, and good macho talk while you're hanging out with your boys, but are you cheating yourself? Are people with vital bits of information simply bypassing you?

There are thousands of ways to gain information, some work for some people and not for others. Figure out what works and when it works for you. Ideally, you want to become an "information magnet."

Understand that in being an information magnet, information must run in two directions. It can't be "Give it to me, and I give you nothing." You won't stay in business very long, or at least not effectively.

In the process of becoming an information magnet, you begin to learn who the other "magnets" are and work to develop a solid relationship with those people. That is how to develop your "network."

It sounds easy, but it's not, and it takes time and effort. But it is worth it.

Information is important because it could save your life or the life of someone you care deeply about. Think about that as you're doing your job. The more you know, the better off and safer you are.

"No Matter How Hard You Tell Yourself You 'Are' Or 'Aren't' Going To Work, What If A Rattlesnake Jumps In Your Lap?"

The problem with police work nowadays is attracting the "right" type of people that want to do the job for all of the right reasons. This means attracting people that are dedicated to making society a better place for everyone to live in everyone. We are talking about having more dedication than the average person out there going about his or her life in their own way.

With all of the "defunding the police" talk now popular among certain people, politicians, and police critics, it's no wonder that police officers, in general, are a little more hesitant to do their job in a proactive manner. It's a hard-enough job protecting society anyways without the added burden of carrying along the criticism of those who seem to be looking over your shoulder all of the time.

You can avoid criticism if you choose to do very little or nothing. The problem with that is by carrying around that "do-little" attitude you eventually let your guard down. You are preparing yourself to "do little" or "do nothing," so your mental preparation that goes into getting yourself ready for the shift will suffer. It can't help but suffer because you are expecting to do less with your time.

I would normally try to get myself ready no matter what I was working on patrol, detectives, or whatever assignment I might have for that day. I always tried to be prepared for whatever might come my way because I also had other officers depending on me as I depended on them.

In fact, one of the true fears I had while on the job was the fear of letting my fellow officer down and allowing him or her to be seriously injured or killed. Luckily that never happened.

My point of this little message is that even if you think everyone is doing it, you never really know what life has in store for you and what is up ahead. Prepare for the worse, and even if you work in the "quietest" and/or "slowest" town in your region, you will be ready when shit happens. Assume it will. That is really the mark of a competent, professional law enforcement officer because you are paid to handle whatever may come your way … good, bad, pretty, or ugly.

I just really want you to be alert and not be caught napping … when you shouldn't have to be told that.

Remember, the rattlesnake is out there.

"The More You Know, The Less People Lie."

If you're doing things right in your career, you should be getting better and better as time goes on. The job is all about communication and how you deal with people.

If you show respect, you're more likely to get respect in return. It's not a gang or gang culture thing; it's a people thing. The only difference is with a gang member; disrespect can get you killed right on the spot.

Also, with gang members, suspects, and/or criminals, a certain amount of respect comes across as self-confidence on your part. If you display a certain level of self-confidence, it tells whoever you're dealing with that you know your job, you understand what you're doing, and you can probably take care of yourself.

Criminals tend to feel that the average cop is pretty much a "square" who can be lied to because they lack the street instincts to know when they are being hoodwinked. It may be in your conversation, your body language, or how you generally carry yourself, but if the person you are dealing with believes that you know your stuff, they will tend to lie less.

"Just Because You Think Someone Is A Punk Doesn't Make Them A Punk."

In 1988 and 1989, I addressed the University of Southern California Trojan football teams, giving the players insight into how life was in south/central Los Angeles especially concerning the gang problem.

Larry Smith was the football coach, and I had a couple of good talks with him. He wanted the players to be aware of the issues involved in wandering off campus to socialize. Many of his players were not from Southern California and did not know the areas of the city to stay away from.

The first time I addressed the team was memorable for me because Junior Seau was getting a good ribbing from some of the players for something he had done at practice. He took it well, and it seemed he was a great guy that was good for the team and in the locker room. I would realize years later that this happened to be the Hall of Famer Junior Seau.

A key message I shared was that looks can be deceiving. I described a scenario in which a couple of them are out late, grabbing some food at the local Fatburger, where everyone goes for some late-night grub. You're standing in line and accidentally bump into some teenage kid half your size. The kid is upset about the bump and wants to make a big deal about it. On the inside, you're laughing because you know you can squash this "punk" like a grape. Despite the obvious size and strength advantage and the fact there are three of you, this kid is still not backing down. Why is that?

I go on, "he is not backing down because, based on his hostile, trouble-making attitude, he is probably a gang member who is carrying the 'equalizer' in his waistband and wouldn't think twice about capping your ass, especially to avoid getting his butt whipped."

I ended this particular lesson with some advice, "Just because you think someone is a punk doesn't make them a punk."

As I use the term "punk" in training and in connection with this part of the book, I refer to the Merriam-Webster Dictionary definition of "a usually petty gangster, hoodlum, or ruffian." To me, this is someone trying to be rough, tough, and significant, but who really isn't? In this context, it is demeaning, so you are really putting the individual down by thinking or referring to them as a punk.

When working in law enforcement, it can be very easy to elevate yourself in your mind regarding your proficiency, tactics, and decision-making skills and assume everything will turn out fine because it usually does. We know this is not true, and things happen.

To operate at a top level, keep mentally, physically, and emotionally prepared for all challenges. But even with all of your preparation, you will cheat the odds of coming out on top if you underestimate your opponent. Like the big, hulking USC football player standing in line at Fatburger staring at an irritated teenager half his size thinking, 'This guy is a punk,' you are placing yourself at risk.

Many years ago, I was speaking at a gang symposium in Chiapas, Mexico, and I had the pleasure of meeting a priest who was operating a "safe house" in Honduras for gang members that wished to leave gang life. The safe house existed because many of those gang members were tattooed all over their faces, which made them a target for fellow gang members who were upset they left the gang, the rival gang members who were still rivals, law enforcement personnel hunting down gang members and vigilantes who believed in taking the law into their own hands. Those gang members and their families had to hide somewhere.

The priest facilitated the safe house for many years and came into contact with hundreds of gang members and their family members. He interviewed most of them, and based on those interviews, he told me a horrendous statistic. He estimated at least 70% of the gang members he dealt with had been sexually molested and/or abused as children. He believed the number was higher, but some of the gang members interviewed were too ashamed to admit being victimized.

He explained that these gang members came to him as "very broken individuals," and he meant broken on many levels. He then gave me a bit of advice to pass on to my American friends in law enforcement. He has met some of the most dangerous people in the world, and they are those who have no hope and nothing to lose. In his words, the most dangerous person is one with nothing to lose."

And if you don't know the individual, you don't know what he is capable of. As an officer, you might be standing over someone half your age lecturing him and have no idea who you're talking to. That kid might be one of those broken people with no conscience or sense of guilt. That kid could be deadly to you if the opportunity ever presented itself.

This is the reason why those professionals that have worked in gangs for some time dislike the term "wanna-be." When you call someone a "wanna-be," you might tend to underestimate him. At what point is that 14-year-old possible gang member no longer a wanna-be? When he runs from you and fires a shot at you, narrowly missing your head? Is he still a wanna-be?

When doing your job, be attentive, vigilant, and sharp. But don't make the mistake of assuming that someone is punk because they might surprise you, and tactically speaking, we don't like surprises.

"When You Watch Cop Reality Shows On TV, Do It With A Critical Eye. Some Of The Mistakes Cops Make Aren't Really Mistakes ... They're Habits. Know The Difference ... Your Life Might Depend On It."

It's nice that because of shows like "Cops" and "Live PD," the people of America are able to see how difficult the job of being a cop actually is. The problem with some of these shows is that it's also a good chance to see how some law enforcement agencies are lackadaisical in their approach to tactics and training. Good tactics and training should be an "ongoing" process. That means that no matter how successful you are, there might always be a better way to handle a problem or situation. That search to get better is a "must" with today's frontline officers, whether you work on the streets or in an institution. That's why we have a "de-briefing" process in law enforcement. There might always be a better way.

The problem with some of the tactical mistakes we see on "reality cop" television shows is that they aren't mistakes at all … they are bad habits.

I will now point out fourteen of them with a bonus tip at the end of this section in an effort to keep all of us alive and well. I'm on your side, and if you can't accept any life-saving tips, that's a "you" problem. I'm here to make you think about it.

TOP 15 TACTICAL MISTAKES … OR HABITS – "REALITY COP SHOWS"

1. **Not Controlling the Suspect(S)** – To me, the concept of "officer safety" means "control." That is what Officer Al McGilvray taught me in my first year out of the academy. The more control you have, the safer you are … simple.

2. **Get Out Of The Car First** – When you pull a vehicle over, and you're going to contact the driver for any reason, you always … always … always get out of your car first. Never ever allow the driver in the vehicle you are stopping to get out first. Get out first and face whatever comes your way.

3. **Walking Up On A Vehicle** – When you do stop a vehicle and are walking up to it, always clear the back seat or rear portion of the vehicle before you proceed. Try to visually look and see what is back there, and if you can't, try bringing the driver back to you until you can "clear" it.

4. **Standing In Or With Back To Traffic** – When or around parked vehicles and traffic, never stand in or with your back to traffic. The traffic and where you stand should always be on your mind. Sometimes it's just a matter of changing up the angle of where you stand.

5. **No Or Substandard Searches** – Searches are for a reason. It doesn't matter how it looks, or if you're in a hurry, there are a lot of bad or substandard searches going on out there. You normally don't realize how bad your searches are until you miss a gun or other weapon on a search. By then, it's too late …somebody failed.

6. **Allowing Suspects To Smoke** – I've never smoked, so it's a lot easier for me to tell someone they can't smoke or to put the cigarette out while I'm conducting business with them. A cigarette in your eye is not fun ... period.

7. **"Rat-Packing" The Suspect's Vehicle** – This usually happens at the end of a pursuit when an officer's adrenalin is going crazy. Everyone wants to be the first one to get the suspect out of the vehicle. Understandable but a tactical nightmare in the making. Exercise self-discipline if you can take your time.

8. **No Cover Or Concealment** – I remember seeing a good example of this in a situation that occurred in Northern California. Two officers were approaching a bank on a "robbery in progress" radio call with armed suspects inside the back. One of the officers was using her partner as a shield as they

approached the bank. Especially with armed suspects, do not needlessly expose yourself or your position. You make the situation worse.

9. **One Officer Chasing Numerous Suspects** – Foot pursuits are difficult tactical situations to experience and can lead to the worst issues, including harm to yourself. Know why you are running after a suspect if the odds are in your favor and if it is worth it. Many times, it is not.

10. **Not Cuffing Up Fast Enough** – Handcuffs are an excellent tool if you can use them. It's the totality of the situation you have to read, but it's easier to take them off if you need to than to get them on in the middle of chaos.

11. **Not Sensing The "Red Flag" …** The Verbal Chaos – When a person starts to talk too much, too soon or isn't making logical sense, that should put you on "high alert." It could be a distraction from what is about to happen.

12. **Creating Crossfire Situations** – This probably happens more than we realize and is a fluid situation, constantly changing. Always be aware of where you put yourself and your vehicle.

13. **Gun Hand Occupied** – Always be cognizant of where your gun hand is and what's in it. Sometimes officers walk up to cars at night with their flashlights in their gun hand looking at the people in the car and not realizing what they are doing. Keep your gun hand free.

14. **Standing In Doorways** – Another very bad habit, especially when you consider how many times officers walk up on houses, especially on radio calls. Also, be aware of windows which can also be as bad as doors.

***** Bonus tip for "real gang cops" *****

15. Familiarity – I say this is especially a liability for a good street cop or gang cop the people that really know their stuff. It can also be the probation or parole officer that knows their caseload or correctional officers that know their institution and inmates. Your knowledge can work against you because it can lull you to sleep, making you complacent.

"Even monkeys fall from trees ..." – Japanese Proverb.

"When A Suspect Looks In Your Eyes To See What's Inside, You Better Hope He Sees A Warrior."

A controversial issue for law enforcement is the "warrior" versus "guardian" concept. There are those who believe that an officer's "warrior" mindset gets him into trouble and creates real problems in the officer's dealings with the public.

They believe that starting in the police academy as an officer taught survival techniques, and a part of that is the officer's warrior mindset. They believe that mindset is harmful in dealing with the public and that today's officer lacks "emotional intellect." So they push a philosophy of de-escalation and make the officer's safety a secondary concern.

For a police executive to tell a group of officers to "dump the warrior mentality" and adopt a "guardian" mindset is demeaning and lacks insight. During a normal shift, a patrol officer will wear many hats depending on the situation.

That officer may be a counselor, teacher, parent, adviser, referee, babysitter, mediator, and/or coach.

"Warrior" and "guardian" are just two more of the many roles the frontline officer must fulfill.

The bottom line is these academics and executives aren't going to be with you when entering a residence to deal with a family dispute and a house full of angry people. They will be home sitting by the fireplace and sipping on a choice glass of wine.

If you don't make it out of that house alive, it must have been something YOU did wrong. It certainly wasn't due to their enlightened philosophy and training.

I don't believe an officer's safety should be placed in jeopardy due to some academic insight, especially when the philosophy comes from people who have never done the job or at least not as extensively as many frontline officers have.

Law enforcement managers, academic experts, and politicians examine, critique, and control their officers as much as they want. The problem with enlightened training is the minds designing it can't account for the actions of the people officers deal with.

They are too busy telling an officer how to think, when to think, and what to think. It's creating "paralysis by analysis."

Time after time, there are examples of how an officer's warrior mentality has helped them through perilous situations and kept them alive. Use discretion, experience, and logic to figure out how to handle the situation you know nothing about until experiencing it.

You must have that warrior spirit inside and be ready for when you need it.

There will come a time when a suspect will decide whether to cooperate or take you on. That decision will be determined by what the suspect sees in your eyes. Let's hope the suspect always sees a warrior.

"Don't Confuse Education With Intelligence ... And Never Confuse Intelligence With Common Sense."

I don't have anything against formal education, and I have learned over the years that you can't judge people based on their formal education, not in police work anyways.

When I was a training officer, I had a recruit that I was training who had only been out of the academy for two months. He apparently was having trouble with his first training officer, so sometimes the department would change things up, especially if a training officer had the reputation of being a "hard-ass."

Like any other relationship, the training officer and the recruit, or as we called them, "probationers," involve humans, so some are better than others. The training officer can be strong, weak, tough, unreasonable, fair, or unfair. The worst ones were too consumed with their own egos and, somewhere along the way, forgot about their job to develop and train a young officer.

The best ones never lost sight of that goal and worked hard to make their probationer competent mentally, physically, tactically, and emotionally. The best Field Training Officers (FTOs) take great pride in their work and great pride in their probationers. You want that probationer to be ready to handle working alone or with other less seasoned officers.

The one thing that stood out to me when I was a training officer was how well the probationer was able to sense danger and react to it.

It's actually "common sense," and working in Los Angeles, it was more like "street sense."

Criminals can size up a probationer or "new cop" by how they look and act. A new cop looks new with a fresh new uniform, is clean-shaven, has kind of "stiff" body language, and is very formal in how they talk to people.

That's why gangsters or criminals will try to engage them in conversation to get a feel for the new cop's comfort level. Usually, the more time you have on the job, the more relaxed or informal the conversation gets because the officer begins to get a feel for what is appropriate and what isn't.

My probationer partner and I once had three gang members stopped, and they were facing a wall as I was going to search them. My probationer was guarding my back as I began the search. All of a sudden, some other gangster came walking up to where we were conducting our business and was going to walk right through the area where I was searching, and my partner was guarding ... a no-no. My partner says to the passive invader, "What the fuck are you doing? Go around!" The invader stopped and went around us.

That had caught the invader's attention, got my attention, and got the gangsters I was searching's attention. He caught the invader's attention because he didn't expect the new guy to step up and take control. The probationer saw that the invader was about to invade our space and prevented it.

He did the right thing in that situation.

That probationer had a high school education, no college, and started working when he got out of high school until three years later when he entered the police academy. He was also born and raised in south/central Los Angeles. His only major problem was that he couldn't spell to save his life.

Luckily, I knew that he wouldn't have to. I got him a little pocket dictionary, and we worked on that issue.

Another probationer I had possessed a master's degree in education, and to this day, I don't know why he wanted a career in law enforcement. He was highly intelligent but couldn't tell a rattlesnake if it was wrapped around his leg rattling. He was a real smart but wasn't wired that way … no "street sense." That would be something we would need to work on, but it's not that easy to do. I could point it out to him, but he would need to acknowledge it and try to work on it himself.

He could learn slang words, watch body language and try to be more self-aware of his surroundings, but it's much easier to be raised in an environment where you are immersed in the factors that determine your safety and well-being. You grow up conditioned to those factors, so you learn it. Call it "street sense" or actually common sense.

Both probationers worked on their weaknesses, and one eventually became a solid training officer and the other a successful sergeant. I'll let you figure out which was which.

Don't confuse education with intelligence, and never confuse intelligence with common sense.

And if you are one of the "educated" ones, don't forget that because it could save your life one day.

"Be Ready ... This Could Be 'Game Day.'"

Back in the middle '80s, when I was driving the yellow "Pac-Man" police car, I'd have to say that life was good. I had been on the job for ten years now and had been in the gang unit for 3 ½ years.

The year before, in 1984, we had discovered and broken up a plan by some gang members to rob a busload of Olympic tourists headed up to the Los Angeles Memorial Coliseum. That saved the city some embarrassment, and although we didn't receive any medals or commendations, we averted a major, worldwide incident because the 1984 Olympic Games were being held in Los Angeles at the time.

My partner and I had also made some solid arrests putting some major gang members away and off the street for various violent and criminal acts. I had also been conducting gang training and helping other officers in that way. I was getting comfortable doing that, and I really liked it. I also started to get requests for my training, and that made me feel good and rewarded. I didn't need awards and medals because my peers knew who was solid and authentic.

We shared a squad room on the third floor of Parker Center with four other units, one of them being the Special Investigation Section (SIS). SIS, as they were known, had the job of following "possible" robbery suspects until they committed a crime, usually a bank robbery. They were also used in cases where kidnappings occurred, and there was going to be a ransom drop. There were good at that, too.

Back then, Los Angeles was known as the "bank robbery capital of the world" because so many had occurred on a regular basis in the city. This was also probably because there were so many banks.

So, when a bank robbery occurred, the suspect(s) normally got away, but sometimes there was evidence or clues left behind. When the clues were not enough to arrest somebody but may have been enough to "lead" or "suspect" someone, SIS would follow the potential suspect until a crime was committed or the suspect didn't do enough to continue the surveillance.

Many bank robbers are "serial" in nature, meaning they commit more than one or commit them on a regular basis.

As you can imagine, those guys had more than their share of officer-involved shootings because when somebody actually goes into a bank to rob it, they are usually armed with a weapon of some kind. Bank robbers are also ready to use their weapons on any "hero" that wishes to intervene in their crime.

As far as any plainclothes unit in the LAPD was concerned, SIS was the epitome of tactics and training other units compared themselves to. As you can imagine, SIS was constantly training their detectives in shooting, tactics, and driving.

We would see their personnel every once in a while, in the office, but they spent most of their time in the field. One day, one of their investigators was in the office and told me that he wanted to have a word with me. I said, "Of course," and we sat down at my desk.

This guy we'll call "John" was one of the true warriors of that unit, having been involved in numerous shootings and all of them "good shootings." I've been around many, many cops, and many of them walk around like "Dirty Harry," trying to portray the image of a "stoned killer" with the ego of a "rock star." I had known "John" casually for a couple of years, and I knew his background. He was the "real deal," but he was quiet and unassuming.

I never spoke much to John, so this little talk was kind of surprising to me. I figured he must have a question about gangs, or he needed a favor or something.

John looked me in the eye and said, "Are you ready for what's headed your way?" That kind of puzzled me, and I didn't know how to answer him.

He then added, "I see how you walk around, and I know you love your job. I also see how successful you are, but I just want to make sure that you and your guys know what's up ahead."

I got it now. John saw me as a meteor headed toward Earth with not enough regard for how or where I may land. He sensed something in me that even I didn't realize. I have to admit that at that time, I never thought about losing or not being successful. I understood the challenges and dangers of the job, but I might have had the "that won't happen to me" syndrome. This was one person caring about another person enough to dial him back and help him to refocus on the job itself. If this didn't come from a person like "John," I would not have understood or received it very well. I had too much respect for John, and I listened to every word. John never spoke very much.

His last words were, "I just want to make sure that you're ready."

Two weeks later, we were involved in a shootout with a gang member wanted for murder who got one shot off with a Mac-10. He was shot and killed by other officers in our unit. I struck his vehicle with my yellow "Pac-Man" police car twice as he was trying to get away, which led up to the shooting.

Days later, when I had a chance to clear my mind on a few things, I thought back to my talk with John.

He knew we were headed for something like the shooting because he could sense it. As well as I thought I knew my job, I didn't sense it coming or care enough about it. I knew the possibility was always there, but I really wasn't aware enough to think that it would be me getting into the shooting and how I would react to it immediately after. I thought that things would turn out "right" like they normally do.

I've been involved in sports my entire life because my dad promoted sports with me. I played little league baseball, played Pop Warner football, and one year of football in high school. I wound up playing varsity basketball also in high school, so I knew what being in a "big game" meant.

When you play team or individual sports, you know when a "big game" is coming, and you prepare, prepare and prepare for it. You prepare so that you can rise to the occasion and defeat your opponent when the time comes.

You don't have that luxury in police work.

You don't get a heads-up for the "big game" in police work. You don't get a chance to prepare for that special moment, so you need to be "ready to go" at a moment's notice. You have to be mentally, physically, and emotionally ready to go because you won't get a week or two to prepare for that moment. You won't get a date and time for that moment.

If you are focused and aware enough to make it past one of the job's "big games," there's always the next one. That might happen a year or two later, or it could happen the very next time you work. It could happen when you are off the job. You won't know.

Your job is to act like it's "game day" and be ready. Someday you'll look back and think about the things that didn't happen because you were ready for the "big game."

Like the saying goes, "better to be a warrior in a garden than a gardener in a war".

"What Kept Me Alive? ... My Situational Awareness."

Situational awareness is keeping track of where, who, and what is around you and what is happening in your immediate environment. It is your current surroundings and being aware of your own capabilities so that you can react to sudden changes in those surroundings. The people that know this better than anyone are those of you who work in correctional facilities.

Back in 1985, I worked with the Los Angeles County Sheriff's Operation Safe Streets (OSS) gang unit in the LA County Jail. They gave me a desk in their office, and I wore my navy-blue LAPD raid jacket while I was working in the jail. We can say that I stood out because, at that time, I was the only person working in the entire jail and wearing a blue LAPD raid jacket.

After the first week of wearing that jacket, the Crip and Blood modules got used to it, and it wasn't a big deal in the jail amongst the inmates. As you can imagine, the LAPD didn't have many fans in the LA County Jail. My head was always on a swivel, checking out who was around me and what they were doing. On some days, even when it was uneventful, I'd go home pretty drained because it took a lot of energy to constantly engage inmates and keep track of my surroundings. My safety depended on situational awareness.

I've talked to quite a few officers who have been shot and/or involved in deadly confrontations with suspects. I have also experienced a few myself, and the consensus that carried many of them successfully through the situation was thinking about that type of situation beforehand, thinking about those types of situations, and being mentally prepared.

I coached Little League baseball for a few years, and one of the best drills was creating situations with base runners and setting up the players on the field. I might have runners on first base and third base, and one out. Then I would ask various players on the field, "If the ball is hit to you, what would you do?"

The next situation might be a runner on third base and nobody out. What would you do? Because each player could analyze the situation before the ball was hit to them, they could make their decision with less anxiety and confusion. It also gave them the confidence to know that they were ready to make the play. It was an effective way of working on their "situational awareness."

The best advice I can give is to constantly work on situational awareness. As you gain experience and add that experience to common sense, alertness, tactical proficiency, and knowledge, you will become more prepared.

Recognizing a situation as it plays out and being aware of one's own capabilities will assist in making the best tactical decisions and staying alive. I have gone through a million situations in my head, even after I retired, and it is never a waste of time.

As well-known author and Crip gang member "Monster Kody," Scott once told me, "There are two kinds of cops. There's the one that if you punch him in the face and he sees his own blood, his brain will melt down, and he'll freeze up. Then there's the other kind that when he sees his own blood, he gets mad, and the fight is on."

The second kind of officer knows that just because he may be bleeding, he is not defeated, and the fight is not over. Be the "fight is still on" kind of person.

Chapter 6 – You and Your Battle

"If you're no good to yourself, you're no good to anyone else."

- Unknown

"We Are Not All Broken ..."

I read an article, and I have to say it pissed me off.

It was about "police suicides," and it implied that the problem had gotten so out of hand that it looked like all of us in law enforcement were destined for the "darkest of days."

I don't believe our careers always lead to darkness and tragedy, with the rewards never outweighing the damage. Sure, there are setbacks and even tragedies, but it is not necessarily our fate. That is also the challenge of the job.

Again, I'm not underscoring the drama and tragic events that come along with a law enforcement career. I am saying that there is a certain amount of joy, satisfaction, pride, and honor that also comes along with the job, or no one would take the job, to begin with.

There are also some great perks like adventure, challenge, teamwork, camaraderie, social interaction, and of course, many types of personal success. Sometimes you win the little battles no one even knows about, but they count.

As in all walks of life, the bad parts are there alcoholism, addiction, PTSD, stress, medical issues, mental illness, violence, and death, to name a few.

I think what gets to a lot of law enforcement officers, in particular, is the feeling that we in the profession, whatever facet or position that may be, aren't appreciated enough for what we do. I have seen it over the years and felt that way myself on occasion.

But then I have to ask myself why I came into the profession, to begin with. I like being outside, and I like adventure. I was raised as an athlete, so I really like being part of a team and the camaraderie that comes with it.

I like doing something honorable and being respected by my parents, family, and friends. I also like kids, and I don't like "bullies" and bad people, which the world seems to be full of. I also like making decent wages and having security for my family and myself.

What really motivated me to be a cop was that I wanted to do something that not just anybody else could do. Being a cop, I'm not just talking or acting like I am making a difference; I'm actually making a difference. I've never been one who is impressed with a lot of talk. If you're going to talk the talk, be the talk.

A big part of a law enforcement career is the peer pressure.

It doesn't matter if you are a uniform cop, correctional officer, probation or parole officer, the tasks are different, but the peer pressure is there.

I just hope most people are strong enough not to let peer pressure weaken them or convince them that all is negative. It's really prevalent in law enforcement, and you really notice it when you become a supervisor. You have to keep your people disciplined and in line but also try to keep them happy.

There are just some people who want to be negative and who want to look for bad stuff to happen … so they can be right, and things can be bad.

I loved police work and tried to maintain that attitude throughout my career. I found that with a healthy attitude, when bad things do happen, you deal with those issues and try not to let them "infect" the rest of your life or the lives of those around you. It's not easy, but with most things, it is possible.

Even with injury, disease, or death, I tried to be "positive," which in those cases means you are strong or stronger than most. I'm not a doctor, but I can be there for others for advice, support, or just to let them know you are there. I've been on the downside of those times and know how much it means.

I think if there is something we can do better in law enforcement is to be there for each other. You don't have to be an official resource for someone who just needs another person to lean on. If you are a good person to others, you are good whether they need you or not. You can be the light for someone temporarily stuck in darkness … because that happens to everyone. I just don't think we need to live or exist in darkness.

That becomes a habit.

So, when I hear stories about others in law enforcement that have experienced tragedy or despair firsthand, I really feel for them because they are my brothers and sisters. But when someone says something like "we are all broken" or "the job will never love you back," I have to take issue with that. That's not true, but some will buy into it because they want to be accepted by their peers.

One of the challenges of a career in law enforcement is to avoid the obstacles and pitfalls you will encounter in your career, and you will encounter them. Try to minimize the effect of those challenges with a strong, positive mindset and not believe everything you hear. Over a 25-30-year career, you will be glad you did.

You will be better overall by having a strong, positive mindset ...

People eventually care who you are ... not what you are

I used to give academy recruits training on gangs. The recruits would get the gang class a week before graduation, and by then, they already knew what division they were being assigned to. I would normally get questions about specific gangs in specific divisions because a lot of the recruits wanted to know what they were stepping into, gang-wise.

During a break at one of the classes, a very attractive, blonde female recruit introduced herself, "Excuse me, Detective Moreno, I'm being assigned to Hollenbeck Division, and not being a Latino or speaking Spanish, I don't think I will be accepted very well there."

Hollenbeck roughly covers the East Los Angeles area, and its residents are probably 90% Hispanic. I grew up in Hollenbeck Division.

This recruit had a look on her face of grave concern, but little did she know she was setting up a false barrier for herself; already thinking she didn't fit in and she wasn't even there yet. I spoke to her as if she was one of my daughters being tossed into that situation.

I explained when she leaves the academy and goes to her new assignment; she will develop a new reputation. I say "new" because one has already been developed in the academy. A new assignment usually results in a fresh start with a new reputation.

Whether it's due to work quality, ability to learn and grasp new information, handling oneself in stressful situations, and/or following instructions, you will develop a reputation with peers, superiors, training officers, citizens you encounter, and the suspects you deal with, including gang members.

You also have the added curse of being an attractive woman, so try not to let that get in the way. In a way, you might be "overly accepted." As far as your femininity is concerned, other female officers are already working there, so learn how they handle themselves in various situations, both in and out of the station. You will find some exceptional female officers who will help with any issues you might have.

As you develop your reputation, you really want to be known as fair, courteous, strong, courageous, smart, wise, and someone who takes care of business. Be a cop who knows her stuff.

The secret, especially with gang members, is they care who you are, not what you are. Part of being a gang member is that law enforcement is constantly sticking their nose in their business. Understanding that is part of being a gang member, they would rather deal with specific officers. It could be because a certain officer treats them better, they think they have a certain officer snowed so they can take advantage, they may believe an officer has more influence or "juice," or they might just want to stay on a particular officer's good side to use him later on.

My point is that it may have nothing to do with ethnicity, religion, gender, or race. It has to do with who you are and how you do your job. It has to do with how approachable you are, how much you are respected, and how "sharp" you are perceived to be … in other words, how much you know your stuff.

I was a Latino officer born and raised in a Latino family and immersed in Latino culture, yet I developed myself into one of law enforcement's foremost experts on Crips and Bloods … black street gangs, and I'm not black.

The one true obstacle can be a language barrier, but outside of that, don't create more hurdles. It's bad enough that everyone you come into contact with, both those wearing a badge and those not wearing a badge, will be judging you. Don't create even more barriers for yourself.

It's all about how you do your job and how you treat people … simple as that.

"Loyalty to yourself, first."

A very long time ago, when I was a kid, my father took me aside and had a talk with me about loyalty. He made it easy for me by putting it in the context of team sports.

I had grown up a Los Angeles Angels baseball fan, not a Dodger fan. Back then, the Angels would sign autographs after the game, but the Dodgers wouldn't, or at least that was my perception. Even when the Dodgers were winning a couple of World Series, I didn't waiver. I had my connection to my team, win or lose.

My dad said, "You see how you like the Angels no matter what, and you don't like the Dodgers? That's good because you are loyal. You won't change your team just because things aren't going good. You want to be like that when you get older because it's a good thing to be. Not everybody is loyal." I kind of got what he was saying, and I kind of didn't.

Flash forward a few years, and our discussion on loyalty continued. My dad said, "You're going to meet a lot of people in your life, some good and some bad. Some people you will get very close to, and others are just passing through. Some people you will trust, and they will help you, while others will disappoint or hurt you. The point is that no matter how much you trust or care for someone, they can always turn on you. That's why you always save a little piece of you for yourself. Always be loyal to yourself."

He didn't mean to enjoy love, intimacy, companionship, or friendship. He meant that the most important person in the world to you should be you. No matter what happens, even if everyone were to turn their backs on you, you still have you. That is the most important thing.

And as you go through life, you can pick out those who are more loyal to you than others. You learn over time and through experience. Even then, you can still be wrong about someone, so that's why you remain loyal to yourself.

Don't confuse loyalty with devotion. Loyalty is why someone feels obligated or devoted to you, and I'm not just talking about it in the romantic sense. I'm talking about an obligation that one person feels for another. So loyalty is more of a basis for devotion.

There are a lot of unhappy people out there who seem to have abandoned their loyalty to themselves or never had it. They were never given the opportunity to learn how important they are or can be.

Now, I'm not talking about being selfish. Being selfish is putting your concerns mainly on yourself and to your advantage to the exclusion of others.

When you look up "loyalty" in the dictionary, phrases like "faithfulness to commitments or obligations" pop up.

So being loyal is, in a sense, a giving of you. You give yourself to your mate, your family, your friends, your studies, your job or career, your personal causes, and to everyone else around you.

Much like you would do for your favorite sports team, when times are good or times are bad, you stick with them.

My dad was trying to tell me that it's all fine and dandy to be loyal. But when things go bad, as they sometimes will with you personally, you need to be loyal to yourself. Give yourself the same break that you might give your favorite sports team going through a bad time.

Remain strong and committed in your devotion to yourself.

"Don't Take Everything Personal."

During my career and when I was in the "penalty box" for three years of a large-scale narcotics misconduct investigation, I was assigned to Northeast Division Detectives, an area that covered Highland Park, Eagle Rock. Echo Park, Silverlake, and the East

Hollywood section of Los Angeles. It turned out to be a real good spot to work, and I met some great people while I was assigned there.

One morning I was driving in, and as I drove by the front of the station, I saw that someone had crossed out the sign that said "Los Angeles Police Department" on the front wall of the station. Below it where it said, "Northeast Police Station," and "3353" (the address) was unmarked. Where the police department was crossed out with a painted line through it, "Avenues 1" was placed above it, just like the Avenues gang would do on a rival gang wall.

There was no sign of a suspect, so I drove around to the employee parking lot and entered the detective squad room. When I entered the squad room, you could tell that the cat was out of the bag. Everyone knew the station had been victimized by the "Avenues" gang. The Avenues gang was one of the largest in the area Northeast Division covers and one of the largest in the city. It was a big "fuck you" to the cops working the area, but I had to laugh at what a brazen but cowardly act of defiance it was.

Different detectives had different responses to the graffiti cross-out, but none of them were favorable. Someone slammed his stapler on his desk, others were cussing out the gang and declaring war, and others were outraged by the brazen act of vandalism.

While the general mood of the detectives in the squad room that morning was one of being "pissed off," I took my camera and went outside to get a good photo of it. It was another good slide for my gang presentations. I thought it was a good teaching moment.

To me, it was like a good practical joke. A good practical joke affects different people in different ways. Some people laugh, some get pissed, others don't "get it," while people like me, in this case, laugh at the person creating the joke itself.

I laugh because if you go through life and the best thing you can do is write some gang graffiti on a police station wall, I hope you are only about 12 or 13 years old. Whoever wrote it had the idea of getting back at the cops by pissing them off ... by disrespecting them. It didn't work this time, homeboy. It didn't piss me off. It humored me ... and gave me another photo to make a teaching point in my training.

I actually feel sorry for the person who wrote on the wall because I'm sure that getting away with it was some type of moral victory. But in the life of a young gang member, you've got real challenges up ahead. You have to worry about having a decent mentor or role model and having enough sense to accept what they may give you. You have to worry about your family, your parents (if you have any), your brothers and sisters, your living situation, your financial situation, your schooling, your love life, your gang, cops, the justice system, and whatever you're going to do with your life.

You didn't piss me off, homeboy. You actually amused me. You don't know what's up ahead in life for you, and I do. The joke is on you.

That's why I try to take things "in stride" and try not to make things personal. When you let people get under your skin, they win.

And they might mistake you for some type of "rookie" ...

"Your Career Is Part Of Your Life ... Not The Other Way Around."

Life is a series of phases. School, dating, work, a bill, and a car are all phases and parts of your life.

In law enforcement, it's the same, but it's easy for many of us to get carried away with "the job." We devote so much and make so many sacrifices our job truly becomes our identity, our master status. When we wake up in the morning, that's who we are and what we look forward to. When we go to bed at night, it might be our last thought of, who we are, and what we accomplished that day.

The problem happens when the job becomes your whole life. A law enforcement career can be so unique and unpredictable that we tend to have phases within the phase of our career; different assignments, different partners, different ranks, and specific incidents.

Even with all of those separate phases over the course of a 10, 20, or 30-year career, they are just a part of your life. Not the other way around.

As I was getting close to retirement, people asked, "How are you going to function not being a member of the LAPD?" Most of the people asking knew me only as a cop and couldn't see me otherwise. They didn't realize; like all of us, I have other dimensions to my psyche other than being a cop.

Don't put all of your eggs in one basket. Mentally and emotionally speaking, how do you carry your eggs if your basket breaks? As Mike Tyson stated, "Everyone has a plan until they get punched in the face."

The law enforcement career can be a tantalizing seductress who takes away desire for anything else. That's where the danger is; what happens if your seductress deceives you or, worse yet, totally abandons you?

Over the course of a 25-year career, the job at times may disappoint, discourage, and dishearten you. Put things in perspective and remember that these certain phases are part of a larger phase that comprises your life. There is life beyond your career.

There might be family, good friends, and loved ones, hobbies, and other skills you're involved in, the music you love to hear, and the trips you need to take. There are more phases and dimensions to your life. People that know you will still like and support you whether in law enforcement or not. That's how "normal" people function on an everyday basis, and they're not connected to law enforcement in any way. However, they will never understand how amazing your "seductress" made you feel when the times were good.

Even if she walks out on you, she can't take the memories with her.

"Your Morale Is Your Morale … No One Else's."

In the dictionary, the word "morale" is described as the state of the spirits of a person or group exhibited by confidence, cheerfulness, discipline, and willingness to perform assigned tasks.

A few years ago, while I was still an active member of the Los Angeles Police Department, we were sitting around talking, and the subject of morale came up. One of the guys had a friend that worked in our SWAT Unit, and they had a squad meeting where our

Chief of Police showed up. This was the Chief prior to Chief Bratton's arrival, and the name isn't important.

During that squad meeting, one of the SWAT members asked the question, "Chief, what are you going to do about the morale problem in the Department?" During this time, morale was at a low point, with many of our officers choosing to leave the LAPD for greener pastures everywhere else.

Without hesitation, the Chief answered, "I'm not going to do anything. Morale isn't my problem ... it's your problem."

This unexpected and impersonal answer enraged many of the officer's present, and the word quickly spread of what the Chief had said. As this story got relayed and repeated, more and more officers became upset and disgusted with the perceived arrogant and uncaring attitude on behalf of the Chief.

When I first heard it, I wasn't sure that I believed he had actually said that, especially in the presence of some very seasoned officers. As it turns out, he did say that or something to that effect.

Once I realized that the statement was made to the troops, I was pretty bugged by the comment as well. But the more I thought about what the Chief had said, the more my reaction began to change.

You have to understand that during this time period, I was supervising a squad of 13 detectives whose mission was to seek out and apprehend gang members who had committed violent crimes in the city of LA. This was not a desk job but one requiring investigative proficiency and tactical excellence. At any time and on any day, our squad members faced violent attacks and even death at the hands of the most violent of criminals running amok in our communities. This was not even considering that one mistake or error in judgment during an arrest or takedown situation could wind us up on the front page of the LA Times or on national TV. Obviously, I tried to run a smooth ship with little distraction as possible.

The more I thought about what the Chief had said, the more I began to agree with him, and here is why.

Morale is a very personal issue. The most important factor involved in affecting your morale is you. What that Chief basically said was that if you're going to sit around and wait for him to make you feel better, that isn't going to happen ... and he was right.

And not only is morale important in our professional careers, it is just as important in our personal lives as well. Funny that the word "morale " is never equated or connected to our personal lives, just our work or professional careers. In reality, your morale can affect all facets of your life.

I am writing this article as an old experienced, battle-scarred codger who has been through a multitude of morale-shaking situations and experiences, as many as you can imagine in a 32-year law enforcement career. I have come out on the other end of it, still smiling and laughing and still treasuring my personal morale. I must have done some things right. Here are some bits and pieces of my philosophy on "your morale."

~ You are the most important person.

~   If you don't take care of yourself, you won't be of value to anyone else. When you feel good, you can make others feel good.

~   Sincere and hard-earned knowledge leads to proficiency in your craft. Your talent can be minimized but not taken from you. Your value is always your value.

~   Consistent, good work eventually silences your critics and detractors. I think of myself as a good guy who doesn't go around screwing people over.

~   My professional enemies have always been people who were jealous or envious of me. Usually, when they get a taste of my consistently good work, they fade into silence. It's not a matter of proving anything to anybody. It's a matter of living up to the things that bother your detractors to begin with ... your reputation, your work, and your consistency.

~   Good work makes you feel better.

~   A good arrest, a nice caper, a solved crime, a solution to a tough problem, or a meaningful interaction with a friend or loved one. Things that you do that also reinforce your sense of value within yourself.

~   Avoid negative influences.

~   That really means avoiding negative people. For some reason, a lot of law enforcement professionals especially love to go around pissing and moaning about this and that. We all have had legitimate reasons to complain, no doubt. My issue is with those of us that choose to immerse ourselves in negativity. A part of how you demonstrate character, leadership, and resiliency is how you handle adversity. Do you bounce back? Do you shake it off and continue when you can? Can others depend on you because of your strength? I'm not taking away anyone's right to complain. But if you keep making me look at your scar, after a while, it's no longer very interesting.

~ Your career is only a part of your life, not the other way around. If something does go wrong in your work, you should be wise enough to have your support system already in place. I used to (and still do) have friends for various things or issues. I might confide in this person regarding something to do with work. On a family matter, I might open up or seek guidance from this other person. Customize your support system for yourself. Seek loyalty, honesty, and courage in your support people because that may be what it takes to keep you on track.

~ Your attitude affects those around you. This is magnified if you are a supervisor charged with leading or setting the tone for your group or unit. My best teacher in this was my dad as I was growing up. Never once in all of that time did he ever use the word "stress." It wasn't in his vocabulary. As I got older and became a husband, father, and man, I realized that there were many times when my dad was under a lot of stress. He never let his stressors bleed out onto or affect his family. He handled it himself. He also took great pride in being the traditional provider and protector in his home. My morale as a youngster growing up was great because I never had to deal with or worry about his problems.

Remember what is important to you. I remember being held as a prisoner of war by our Internal Affairs Division for almost three years. During that time, I was under a lot of stress, unable to function as a "normal" officer because I was under suspicion. I was placed on restricted duty and unable to do the things at work that I took pride and pleasure in. I was mad, frustrated and eventually suffered a severe case of Vertigo. With law enforcement officers, injustice really enrages us. I was being treated unjustly. Three things made a difference and helped pull me through

1. When I would complain about the Department's treatment of me, my dad just said, "Are you getting paid?"

When I replied, "Yes," my dad said, "Good. As long as you are able to take care of your family, they can have you doing nothing ... so what."

2. I was walking around all of the time, pissed off at what was going on with me. To me, my problem was the most important issue in the world. Then one day, I was exiting the men's room at a pizza parlor when a young boy about 8 years old entered at the same time. He needed me to help him with the door because he was unable to walk without the use of some very large braces on both of his legs. He thanked me, and that basically floored me. This kid had real problems, and I was wandering around, obsessed with my own issues. He was much worse off than I. That adjusted my perspective.

3. My youngest son Marcus was about 7 years old, and I would go home and watch TV with him. He'd lean against me, and whenever he touched me, it was like an energizing force. It felt good because it reminded me that no matter what happened to me at work, he still loved me, and that wouldn't change.

I wrote this article as a means of reminding you how good we have it. We are involved in dynamic careers and living in the greatest country in the world. We have running water, great food and live diverse lives in a safe, mostly civilized world.

Appreciate what you have. Appreciate those around you. Allow yourself to be happy or at least involved in the search for happiness ... you deserve it.

After all, it is your morale ...

"Anyone Can Be Strong When There Are Cheers And Support. The True Test Is In Your Solitude."

Like a lot of people, I play around on Facebook. I have a lot of Facebook friends, about 800+.

I maintain a Gang Cop Page and also belong to a few "law enforcement only" pages. I can interact and communicate with a lot of people and also see what they post.

I think that Facebook had created a few "types" that didn't seem to be around before it became popular. Before Facebook, people had to call, email, send a letter, or go and find someone to communicate with. Now it's just a matter of turning on your computer and putting your thoughts out there.

I really notice some "interesting" personalities on the "law enforcement only" page. I'm sure that even with law enforcement officers, there is a persona for Facebook and a different persona when that officer is actually working and facing real-life situations, not just posturing to puff up an image for the peer group.

Some officers write posts that anger the other members.

Some write posts to create controversy, to gain support during a tough situation, or to brag about their assignment, their agency, or the case they just made. The response is immediate and can become addicting if you depend on the response of other people.

I post items on a daily basis, but my postings are quotes made to promote thoughts or information regarding officer safety and training issues important to other officers. I've been doing this for a few years, and it helps to keep me current and relevant with the training I provide to law enforcement.

Sometimes I read an item and the responses and think to myself, 'What would they do if Facebook didn't exist?' What if his or her thoughts didn't produce an immediate response from anyone? What did people do for recognition before Facebook?

The answer is that most of us did nothing. You learned to get what you needed as recognition from within yourself, or you learned to go without it. It's great to have support from the people close to you, but what if your issue is something that you'd rather not share? What if it's a situation or a problem that you'd rather not bother others about? I know for me, I'd rather not have people worrying about me, so I kept my mouth shut about a lot of things bothering me.

According to many experts, keeping things that bother you to yourself may not be the ideal thing to do, but it did teach me to try and work things out mentally and emotionally on my own. It taught me not to fear being alone.

I was having a nice talk with my 16-year-old grandson one day, and I told him that one of the greatest fears people have is being alone.

Some people just need to have contact and be around others. You see it in line at the market, you see it while working out at the gym, and you see it at a bar or restaurant. People are more comfortable when they feel connected, so that's why a stranger will talk to you when you're minding your own business.

You can go on Facebook and say things to gain support and cheers from your fellow professionals. You can make bold statements and feel the roar of the Facebook crowd behind you. You can also gain instant sympathy and consolation when you are in the dumps.

You can get a reaction … from many people.

I told my grandson if he can learn to be alone and be comfortable with it, that by itself will put him ahead of a lot of people and help him through life.

Anybody can act and talk big when the cheers and support are there. It's how you are when alone and no one is around. Unfortunately, that is when some people face their darkest hour. People will still love you. People will still care about and respect you. People will even forgive you because no one is perfect.

Be comfortable enough in your own skin to guide yourself through the darkness when you are alone in your solitude.

Being alone is when you can actually be at your strongest.

"Burnout Is Not Always Terminal ... If You Don't Want It To Be."

"Burnout" is a term that has been used through the years to indicate fatigue, unhappiness, sluggishness, or exhaustion with a particular part of a person's life ... usually work.

When I was a recruit in the academy, they would tell us two things ... 1 – "If you're ever involved in shooting, your mind could play tricks on you in the aftermath, so be ready ..." and 2 – "You don't ever want to burn out because then you'll be like the guy up at the academy locker room who passes out towels ..."

I remember those two tidbits of advice like it was yesterday, and they got my attention. I always remembered them.

Years later, I was involved in an officer-involved shooting, and a weird thing happened to me the morning after, and I believed it was my mind playing tricks on me. It turned out to be a really weird coincidence, but a coincidence it was, so my mind was ok. No tricks.

When I thought about the poor guy passing out towels in the academy locker room, I wondered how that guy could find himself in such a rut ... and not want to get out. It was like he was defeated.

"Burnout" can be caused by many things. When you think of the variables involved, no two cases of "burnout" could possibly be the same. We are all different people living different lives, having different dreams, and taking our own different roads in life.

It really comes down to how you react to the things that affect you. No matter how bad things could get for me, I could never believe that I would stay stuck in a burned-out state of mind. At a certain point, I would choose to change my position in life. I think that we always have options.

In training, I use a slide of an example of a very attractive girl approaching you at the gym and commenting to you on how well you look and to "keep up the good work."

My next slide is of a clown with a weird smile and the comment …. "your mind just shifted."

I'm trying to be funny, but I am also showing the power of your mind. A refreshing comment from an attractive woman just slapped you on the head, temporarily jarring your brain and changing your mindset.

So it makes me wonder how much control we actually have over our own mindset because if a stranger can get us into a different mindset, why can't we?

Obviously, things are not always that simple because when you consider all of the negative issues connected with the law enforcement career, it's not as simple as a stranger giving you a compliment. But your mindset or mood is subject to change, and that comes from having the power to control your mind and move on with your thoughts.

In another part of this book, I talk about being in the middle of a lengthy personnel investigation, and I was at a pizza parlor in a mad and brooding mood. I was exiting the men's bathroom, and I noticed someone was attempting to open the door from the outside, which was a little unusual.

I opened the door, and here was a young boy, about 7 or 8 years old, with leg braces struggling to get the door open. I opened the door for him, and he smiled and said, "Thank you, sir."

That smacked me in the head because I thought, here's a young boy who is disabled but still has the time and decency to say "thank you" as I opened the bathroom door for him.

I thought this boy in his situation didn't have the power to fight back his health issues … but I can fight mine. That spun my mind into a different place … a better place. I can fight back as hard as I want to without support or sympathy.

It's my battle, and I can decide how I deal with it. Plus, life happens in phases, and nothing stays the same forever.

"Burnout" can be caused by many factors and can even be a different state of mind for different people, but I think you can fight back. You can change your outlook, change your environment, reflect on the progress you have made in your career, and try to expend your mental energy wisely.

Hopefully, when that beautiful woman walks up to you at the gym and gives you that nice compliment, you have enough composure and self-awareness to smile and say, "Thank you."

"You Can Overdo It With Your Passion …"

I must admit, there were times in my life when I felt the place where I was at my best. The place most suited for me was when I was a young cop working Newton Street Division in south/central Los Angeles.

I felt that was where I belonged. I really loved being out on the street in the middle of all of the radio calls, shootings, and general mayhem. I felt that the people in the community needed us, and being at work and out on the street patrolling energized me thoroughly.

Although there is an inherent danger that comes with the job, I was not worried about being killed or seriously injured. I realized that those were always possibilities, but I was young, confident, and I felt very good at what I did.

I was more concerned with not performing up to a proficient level and letting down my fellow officers. I was more worried about making a mistake and getting someone else hurt or killed. I wasn't overly worried about the danger to me, although I was always aware of it.

One Saturday night, I was at work, and it was real busy, especially the police radio and the constant chatter of calls for service being handed out to anyone that was available to handle them. You could tell by the police radio that all of us were busy … everyone. There were radio calls for fights, shootings, domestic disputes, and other crimes that had just occurred. Our part of the city was going off.

All of a sudden, at about 10 pm, the dispatcher put out a radio call for all available units to meet the watch commander at an address on a long street in an industrial area. All of the businesses were closed. The watch commander is the lieutenant that is in charge of the officers for that particular shift. We were working the PM Watch, and he was the man in charge.

My partner and I proceeded to the location to meet with the watch commander. In all, there wound up being around 7 or 8 patrol units there and about 15-20 officers.

The radio was still crackling with radio calls.

The lieutenant called everyone together and said, "That radio is really kicking our ass tonight. But you know what? Most of you love being out here and in the middle of this. While the average person might think that we are crazy, most of us love this."

He went on, "I just wanted to tell everyone that I appreciate the job you're doing. Just catch your breath and get back at it. Be safe and back each other up out here."

We then all ran off in different directions trying to catch up with the radio calls.

That lieutenant was an old-school-type leader that cared about his people more than he worried about somebody above him looking over his shoulder. He made us take a "time out" so that we would realize that, for some of us, our job was our passion.

He enabled me to freeze time and dissect what I was feeling while out there on a crazy Saturday night. That is when I came to the realization that my job was a passion.

It was something that evoked powerful feelings from within me. My job is where I belong.

I also learned over the years that it's OK to have passion in your life. It's good to have beliefs and causes that you are committed to. But you have to use your passion wisely.

Even though I was a dedicated cop, I had to learn that "too much cop" wasn't good for my family. I also had a wife and three kids at that time. So as the years rolled on, I felt I was able to improve the balancing of my professional life with my family life.

I totally understand how your job or career can become your passion. But you owe it to yourself and your loved ones to balance out your passions. You must also remain passionate about the people you care about and that care about you.

Enjoy your passions while you savor those feelings and experiences. But remember that there can be a thin line between passion and insanity.

"Once Again ... It Comes Back To Your Attitude."

One of the most important weapons that we have in our "arsenal" for life is our attitude. Our attitude can determine whether we succeed or fail, win or lose, progress or digress.

Our attitude is a product of our experiences, perceptions, biases, and mental dexterity. We ultimately decide how we travel our own road, and our attitude is our traveling music.

Our attitude can also burden us with negativity, complacency, and arrogance. In many walks of life, that's a mixture made for trouble, even death.

I was reading a book that had its main topics dealing with the terms paradigm and paradigm shift.

A "paradigm" is basically a model, example, mold, or pattern ... a stereotypical example. A "paradigm shift" is a drastic change in that mold or pattern. The book examines the theory of paradigm shifts within us as individuals.

In other words, for me would mean looking and living outside the "Tony Moreno paradigm" I have created for myself. To myself and a few people close to me, I am predictable in that I think, feel, act and live a certain way. I am the Tony Moreno paradigm, and I will be that way today, tomorrow, and the day after that.

Now in a lot of ways, that's not a bad thing because I happen to think that Tony Moreno is a decent guy most of the time. But maybe I can improve or at least experiment in a couple of areas of my life. You know, try living outside the Tony Moreno box.

Here's a good example of what it means. I love music. I also like to dance but don't have total confidence in it for a couple of reasons. First off, my body isn't made for dancing, and secondly, a good male dancer outshines everyone on the floor because the women swoon over him ... the bastard.

I'm good at a few things, and to me dancing isn't one of them. That's why if I am somewhere and I know I'm going to be dancing, my foreplay sounds like, "Another beer, please."

If I sign up for a ballroom dance class, I am experiencing a "paradigm shift" to the max. I am changing and adjusting the "Tony Moreno paradigm." I am also changing my attitude toward dancing and toward myself.

We all have our experiences, prejudices, perceptions, fears, biases, feelings, and impressions. We all have our attitudes. Sometimes it's good for us to "overhaul" or "check" ourselves. That's how we learn and evolve. That's how we can best experience life itself. You will be the last person to know if you have gone stale. Don't let it happen.

Sometimes you just have to step outside your comfort zone.

See what's there and learn more about yourself. Feeling crappy about lost love? Step outside your paradigm and gain some strength you didn't know was there.

The weight of the world is on your shoulders? A minor change in your attitude … or a paradigm shift can do wonders. You have to get yourself out of your funk ... you do.

So when you are around some friends or loved ones, sit back, smile, look up at the sky, and let out a real loud howl, "Ah-ooh!"

And when someone looks over at you, notices that shit-eating grin on your face and the fire in your eyes, and says to you, "Are you OK?"

You can say, "I'm fine … just checking my attitude." Mental Tactics' are just as important as 'Officer Safety."

It occurred to me that you could be the smartest, best-conditioned, most knowledgeable, and tactically proficient person in the class. But if you go out to your car on a class break and harm yourself because you just found out your significant other is leaving you, then you did not "survive."

I then added some key points to the training addressing the issue of "mental wellness" in regard to "the job." I share some of those points in this article.

In law enforcement, we put much emphasis on tactics and officer safety but not enough on our "mental tactics" on "the job."

"Mental tactics" are important because a "negative narrative" exists that gives the impression there are no benefits or rewards that come from the law enforcement career. It implies law enforcement officers live a "thankless" existence and wind up "broken and damaged."

People all around us in society are "broken," and it's not restricted just to those in law enforcement. I just don't believe that our careers always lead to darkness and tragedy, and the rewards never outweigh the damage. Sure, there are setbacks and even tragedies, but it is not necessarily our fate.

When I entered the LAPD Academy in 1975, I wanted to do a job that most people could not do. I wanted to be "special" in that way. I knew going in that the "highs" would be extremely high and the "lows" dangerously low. In my mind, I was ready for that "rollercoaster" ride.

Two incidents early in my career had lasting effects on me. The first occurred in 1979 when a 4-year-old girl was shot in the chin during a drive-by. My partner and I stayed with her until the ambulance arrived, and I got some of her blood on me. I couldn't believe a human being could do that to a little child, and I was enraged.

At that point, I decided I was going to "terrorize the terrorists" who were terrorizing the community. I was going to do it legally and ethically, but I now knew my personal mission. The little girl survived, and I still have a photo of her from that night as a reminder of the emotions I felt at that time.

The second defining moment for me was when I couldn't get accepted into the CRASH (anti-gang) unit. I knew as much about Crip and Blood gangs as anybody, but I was not allowed in because their lieutenant perceived me as "out of control." I later learned that I made him nervous because I wasn't a "yes person." So I developed a real "chip on my shoulder" regarding working gangs and an appreciation for making my "haters" wrong.

Those two incidents were significant to me because "motivation" is important when you are fighting for your job, your career, or your happiness. Motivation makes you fight harder and isn't always job-related.

One of the best things about "the job" was the people I got to meet, work alongside and form special bonds with. Good or bad, Heaven or Hell, we experienced it together, and that "bonded" us. That bond is the highest form of "love and respect."

I applaud the efforts of law enforcement agencies that address the topics of mental wellness, PTSD, and suicide among its people. However, the real issue is a matter of "trust." Your agency can have remarkable resources in place, but if the employee in question doesn't "trust" the people or the process, he or she won't access the resources.

One drawback is that in many law enforcement jobs, peer pressure is strong, acceptance by your coworkers is vital, and any type of perceived weakness is harmful. Add the fear that disclosing any type of distress to your employer can damage your career and create "shame" for yourself. Your job situation can change, and that itself can compound your predicament.

When people are "not feeling well" about themselves, withdrawing and avoiding others can perpetuate the problem and further promote a downward emotional cycle. Many times, no one notices the inner "struggle."

In the past, when I've felt "down" mentally and not "myself," I would contact one of my "go-to" people and interact with that person. I have different people for different situations.

Those people know me and remind me that I'm capable of overcoming rough patches because I've done it before … like all of us have done.

"FIVE HELPFUL MENTAL TACTICS …"

Hopefully, these five personal tips can be helpful to you as well.

1. Control The "Little Clown" Inside You.

I was once the subject of a widespread corruption investigation. The investigation broke, and I was re-assigned and told not to have public contact. That meant not doing any police work, which was my "love." I was "devastated."

After a couple of weeks of "no public contact," I developed a severe case of vertigo and couldn't even drive.

I saw a city doctor and was cleared of any medical issues. I was then sent to a psychiatrist, figuring it must be "stress." I didn't want to go, but I had no choice. It was "duty-related."

The psychiatrist was an older man who spoke in broken English, so I was skeptical. I explained my situation at work, and he said, "I know your problem. You have suppressed anger. You walk around mad all of the time because you keep saying bad things to yourself over and over."

So basically, I was being my own worst enemy, and we all probably do this more than we realize.

He then told me, "You have to learn to stop doing that. Every time you notice your mind starting to say bad things to yourself, you have to stop it."

He then reached up with his right hand and gave a little whack to the right side of his head with the palm of his hand and said, "Like this … stop it!"

Amazingly, he was right. It worked. But the trick is to catch that "little clown" (as I call him) inside your head when he first starts with the negative talk. Like any toxic relationship, you can control and put a stop to it. If you don't, it can wear you down and make you sick physically, mentally, and emotionally. It can dishearten you and promote a downward spiral in you.

Recently, I was discussing "my little clown" with a mentor of mine who is also retired from law enforcement and a devout Christian. He said to me, "Your little clown is actually 'the devil' trying to weaken you."

I have to admit that does make sense.

2. It's Your Train ... And Your Derailment.

One definition of "derailment" is "the obstruction of a process by diverting it from its intended course." For our purposes, it is something that knocks us off of our routine, program, or regimen. It upsets how we are living our life. It interrupts our "intended course."

As I have mentioned, we do emphasize tactics and officer safety. You need to work on your "mental tactics" so you can get things "back on track." A key component of that could be those "go to" people who will be there for you, whether you like it or not (because it's hard sometimes to accept help).

Sometimes, your "derailment" is merely a "change" of your track and not total defeat or failure. You need to be able to adjust, adapt and get yourself "back on track" or close to it. It can be tiring, but you have to find reasons to maintain your determination, confidence, and your self-worth. That's your competitive spirit.

To me, you get back on track by doing the little things that give you "light and life." Coaching youth sports helped to keep me "normal" and connected to myself. For me, my kids and grandkids have also been great for that.

Everyone is different. For you, it could be music (or a certain song), working out, driving in your car, reading, cooking, or, like me, writing. It's your "mental relief." Sometimes it's just being around certain people who "light you up."

It's your train and your derailment to handle.

3. Life Happens In "Phases."

Your life happens in phases. Things such as your health, your education, your family dynamics, your career, your relationships, and your living situation all occur in phases. Life continues to change and evolve in "phases."

In law enforcement, our assignments, partners, coworkers, supervisors, commanding officers, shifts, and working conditions constantly change and evolve in "phases."

It is important you remember the "phases" because bad things happen that can "distress" and "demoralize" you. You can become "stuck" in a mindset that promotes a feeling of "hopelessness." That "hopelessness" can put you in a downward spiral, wear you down, and defeat you. Hopelessness exists when you lose faith and forget that life happens in "phases" and that everything is temporary.

What has especially worked for me is to avoid piling "negativity on top of more negativity." Too much negativity can make your world a big, bad, dark place and more imposing than it really is. You don't want that.

It's easier to deal with multiple "issues" separately because each "issue" has its own lifespan, and everything is temporary.

Remember, nothing lasts forever. Good or bad.

4. Create Your Own "Circle Of Trust."

What sometimes prevents those in a "distressed" mindset from seeking support is "trust." The person seeking the support needs a "go-to person" who understands their situation and will help to make them stronger and better, especially at that moment.

As "servants of society," we don't want to burden others with our problems. You can overcome that feeling of "burdening others" by having "trust" in a support person who knows you. Trust that whatever you may throw in their direction, they will be honest, understanding, and upright with you. Most of all, they will also appreciate your trust in them.

A "mentor" is "an experienced and trusted advisor." I am in regular contact with a few people who I imagine consider me a "mentor." To me, the honor is in being "trusted" by each of them. Some of these "close friends" I've never met in person. But what is important is the "bond and trust" that exists between us.

And the best part of that "bond and trust" relationship is that it works both ways, and those are people I can turn to.

Build your "circle of trust" and be "trustworthy" to each other.

5. Allow Yourself "Happiness" ... Allow Yourself To Be "Happier."

I read an article entitled "Top Five Regrets of the Dying." All of the regrets of people on their deathbeds seemed logical, but one of them seemed pretty simple and straightforward to me.

The four were basically things like "I wish I had the courage to be true to myself, "... "I wish I hadn't worked so hard," ... "I wish I had the courage to express my feelings," ... and "I wish I had stayed in touch with my friends." I'm sure those are all valid regrets for some people, but they might require a lot of thought. It's tough for me because I tend to be lazy and disorganized.

The last regret was simpler … "I wish I had let myself be happier." I just thought that it was a very sober feeling that didn't take too much thought or effort to reflect on. Just adjust your mindset.

I love pro football, and the LA Rams have been my lifelong team, not because they just won the Super Bowl. Whenever there is a social movement, and the NFL reacts to it, or a player like Colin Kaepernick expresses his negative police rhetoric, someone will decide that all police officers everywhere should boycott NFL football. Well, I like the Rams, so I am still a fan and watch their football games.

I'm not anti-police by any means, but why should someone tell me not to like what I enjoy? To me, it's one of life's little pleasures. Thousands of law enforcement officers across the country have kids who participate in football and other sports. How far do we carry the outrage?

I think for myself, and as long as I'm not doing harm or taking away someone else's rights or pleasures, what's the harm?

By thinking for myself and indulging in this little pleasure, I am happier.

We should probably do more things that make us happier, no matter how small, instead of suffering and trying to be some type of martyr our whole life.

No matter how small it is, I try to make myself happier. That's my goal, and it's probably simpler than it seems.

Think about it and make yourself "happier."

Afterword

Success is relative. What equals success to you may not be the same for the next person. You need to figure out what success means to you because that is part of making yourself happy.

In my younger days, I would walk around saying, "If some gangster happens to take me out, I would have finished so far ahead, it wouldn't even matter."

I meant that I feel I've worked hard and long enough and have done so many "positive" things that some gangster can't un-do what I've already done.

But besides trying to be a good person, good son, good husband, good father, and good grandfather, I've also had a "purpose" in life. I was fortunate to have a "purpose" because it sort of kicked me in the ass whenever I got lazy and unmotivated.

My purpose in life is the "welfare of kids."

In my book, "Cops in America Dealing with the Ferguson Effect," I devoted a chapter to the murders of 53 children across the country due mostly to gang violence. As I was conducting training for various law enforcement and civilian groups regarding my book, a common recurring comment I would get from certain attendees was that I was "focusing on the negative" too much.

A person from a community-based, non-violence group said the training was great, but the group really didn't need to see the photo of a young dead girl in a coffin at the end of the presentation. This was a "professional" person supposed to bring peace to the community, but he and his people "didn't need to see a dead girl in a coffin."

I asked him what his job was and never did get an answer.

I have been conducting training for professional law enforcement officers as well as civilians for over 40 years.

Every time I address a certain group or organization, I think that, in the long run, it helps the future of "our kids." That is what motivates me to keep training people and writing books.

Do you want to know what the "big problem" with our society is? It's the lack of proper parenting. I know because I've experienced and lived it.

I was a happy kid raised in a lower-income neighborhood, but I was happy because I had strong leadership (my dad) and plenty of love (my mom) in the home. I also was not given excuses for my grades or conduct. My dad knew the world wasn't always fair, but if I could read and write, I could go a long way. He was also very responsible for everything going on in the home, and he sacrificed quietly for everyone. That was my example growing up.

I was fortunate, and I realized that and when I became a cop, I tried to give a little extra to the kids I came into contact with because they never had what I had as a solid role model.

Society is rampant with sub-standard or mediocre parenting, but no one can say anything at the risk of being called a "racist." The truth is in the black and brown communities, the crime rate is higher because most crimes are committed by suspect(s) as the same race or ethnicity as the victim. I said mostly, but those are the facts.

That is a BIG problem because no one wants to approach THAT issue.

Adding to my "theory" on crime and juvenile delinquency is that I know and have plenty of black and brown friends who are bringing up decent, law-abiding children because they are "involved" in parenting. They are involved in the upbringing, education, and development of their kids.

Even if they are shared responsibilities, they are still involved. They make sacrifices and prioritize their children before anyone else. It's not a skin problem.

I can't tell you how many times over the years I have heard of a young person involved in a violent crime, and my first thought is, "Where are the parents?" The parents are making excuses for their kids and making excuses for their parenting.

Back in the 1950s and 1960s, parents were held somewhat accountable for what their kids did.

Through the years, that "principle" has eroded severely. If you thought that my dad was going to pay for a window I broke or for some candy I had stolen, you are crazy. That message was ingrained into me at a very young age and has stuck with me my entire life.

I tried to be the same type of parent because that is what I "knew." I could hear of some serious crime in the media and could guarantee that none of my four kids were involved. They were raised to be responsible, accountable, and with no excuses.

Ask corrections and probation people how many of the subjects in their institutions or caseload had a strong role model growing up. The answer will shock you because we were NOT all raised the same way.

"Leaders eat last …" is the quote I used earlier in this book by British author Simon Sinek referring to a key ingredient to "proper leadership."

My solution to most of the problems discussed in this book comes down to my modification of that quote.

"Parents who are always there … eat last."

God bless the kids' parents of this world.

About the Author

Tony Moreno was born and raised in Los Angeles and became a Los Angeles police officer in 1975, spending 32 years in the Department and retiring as a Detective Supervisor in 2007.

During his career, Tony worked a variety of assignments but found his niche working in street gangs, which he successfully did for 20 of those 32 years. He established himself as one of the nation's foremost experts on street gangs and has provided formal training on gangs and related law enforcement subjects for over 35 years.

He is best known as the original "Pacman" from working gangs in South/Central Los Angeles for five years, from 1982 through 1986. During that time, he drove his trademark yellow Plymouth Fury police vehicle. His well-known nickname and yellow Plymouth were later used in the storyline of the classic gang movie "Colors."

Tony has written five other books, 'Lessons from A Gang Cop", "Spinach for the Everyday Warrior," "Cops in America Dealing with the Ferguson Effect," "Pac Man Life" and "Cop Spirit."

He is on the Advisory Board for the California Gang Investigator's Association (CGIA) and the International Latino Gang Investigator's Association (ILGIA).

Tony has two sons in law enforcement and, understanding how important our young people are to our society, has volunteered to coach youth sports for over 20 years.

Find out more about Tony Moreno at www.gangcop.com

Pac-Man Life